Happy
by
Design

Happy

by

Design

How to create a *home* that boosts your *health & happiness*

Victoria Harrison

weldon**owen**

For my wonderful parents—masters of the art of creating a happy home.

Published in North America by Weldon Owen
1045 Sansome Street
San Francisco, CA 94111
www.weldonowen.com

Weldon Owen is a division of Bonnier Publishing USA
www.bonnierpublishingusa.com

This edition published in 2018.

First published in Great Britain in 2018 by Aster,
a division of Octopus Publishing Group Ltd

ISBN 978-1-68188-415-8

Library of Congress Cataloging-in-Publication Data

Names: Harrison, Victoria, 1980- author. | Powell, Debbie, 1982- illustrator.
Title: Happy by design : how to create a home that boosts your health and
   happiness / text, Victoria Harrison ; illustrations, Debbie Powell.
Description: San Francisco : Weldon Owen, 2018. | Includes bibliographical
   references.
Identifiers: LCCN 2018002616 | ISBN 9781681884158 (hardback)
Subjects: LCSH: Interior decoration--Health aspects. | BISAC: HOUSE & HOME /
   Cleaning & Caretaking. | HOUSE & HOME / Decorating. | DESIGN / Decorative
   Arts.
Classification: LCC NK2113 .H35 2018 | DDC 747--dc23
LC record available at https://lccn.loc.gov/2018002616

Printed and bound in China

10 9 8 7 6 5 4 3 2 1
2018 2019 2020 2021 2022

Contents

The Happy Home Program

"I set out to try to find the answer to one simple question: Can our home make us happier?"

Everyone wants to be happy, but sometimes we look for happiness in the wrong places. Wealth, power, and prestige might bring us a short-term boost, but often it is the simple pleasures in life that can bring the greatest level of peace and happiness.

A relaxed alfresco lunch on a sun-drenched summer's day, the cheerful crackle of a roaring log fire, or the quiet peace of your favorite armchair on a lazy Sunday morning—these small moments of domestic contentment are easy to overlook, but maybe we should be focusing on them more in order to boost our well-being.

With stress, anxiety, and burnout seemingly on the rise, I wanted to discover if we could actively improve our health and well-being simply by the way we design our living spaces, and if there were any shortcuts to happiness that we could all embrace. So I set out to try to find the answer to one simple question: Can our home make us happier?

My journey into the science of happiness led me to some fascinating places, from the research labs of NASA to the forests of Japan. As I went along I started to build up a universal Happy Home Program, with the aim of helping everyone create a living space that heals, calms, and nourishes. The resulting book, *Happy by Design*, is packed with tips and inspiration to help you live your happiest life. You can either work right through it, following the full wellness program, or dip in and out for a mini hit of happiness whenever you need it.

By shifting the way we think about our living spaces, from how they look to how they make us feel, I will show you how to create a happy, uplifting home that looks after you from morning to night, and even when you are asleep. Happy reading!

Vicky

1

How to Grow Your Own Fresh Air

How many plants do you have at home? Perhaps you have a succulent in the living room or a peace lily in the bathroom, or maybe a fern gently wilting on a windowsill. But have you ever really given much thought to the impact these humble houseplants could be having on your well-being?

If the answer is no, then it could be time to think again (and show your potted friends a bit more love) because choosing the right plants could be one of the smartest things you can do to boost your health and happiness levels indoors. And the good news? If you already have a peace lily in your bathroom, you are off to a strong start.

Apply Some Rocket Science

If you aren't sure exactly why you should have plants in your home but have just always felt that having some around you is "a good thing," you will be happy to know that you are on the right track. You are also in the company of some very smart people— when I started delving into the world of houseplants, my research led me to a rather surprising place: NASA.

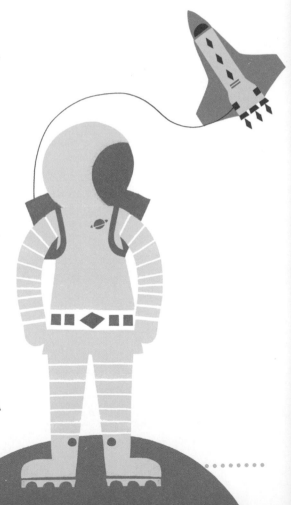

It turns out that indoor plants have been given space-age levels of consideration over recent years, starting in the 1980s when a team of scientists at NASA (National Aeronautics and Space Administration), led by Dr. Bill Wolverton, undertook a Clean Air Study to look at ways of tackling the newly observed phenomenon of "sick building syndrome" (SBS). This condition can occur when a structure is sealed too well and pollutants—released by carpets, furniture, and even cleaning products—build up inside. Think of it as being in a space shuttle, but without the breathing apparatus.

Get some leafy Zen

SBS has been linked to some pretty unpleasant symptoms, such as headaches, dizziness, nausea, and eye, ear, and nose irritation. If you live in a well-insulated modern home, you could be at risk. So, that's the bad news. But on to the good news: NASA found a solution, and it's beautifully simple: Plants. Lots and lots of plants.

I asked Dr. Wolverton just what plants could do for us. "Research shows that just being in the presence of plants helps to reduce stress, lower blood pressure, and, in work environments, increase worker productivity," he says. "Plants also remove airborne volatile organic chemicals (VOCs) and particulate matter." And you might also be interested to know that your plants could be giving you a natural mood boost, too. "They emit negative ions," says Dr. Wolverton, "which not only help reduce airborne microorganisms, but give us a euphoric feeling."

NASA discovered that the best way to detox indoor air is simply to bring in hard-working houseplants. They drew up a list of the top fifty indoor plants for soaking up pollutants, some of which are listed on pages 12 and 13.

What else can plants do for us?

Several scientific studies have revealed that plants in an indoor environment can also lower blood pressure, reduce stress, and impact our overall health in a positive way. Japanese scientist and plant guru Kozaburo Takenaka has spent many years researching just this and developing the concept of "ecology gardens" in hospitals and public buildings. I asked him if he believes that plants can do more than filter the air, and his response was unequivocal: "The ecology gardens not only cleanse the air but they also bring people peace of mind," he told me. "Indoor plants are needed by everyone in the world who aims for clean air and a healthy life indoors."

Pick a Plant, Any Plant

So, how should you choose which plants to have in your home? I asked Kozaburo Takenaka if there are certain plants we should all have in our living rooms or even particular plants for particular rooms, but his advice was surprisingly simple. "I think it's more important to choose plants that match the indoor environment," he said, explaining that plants should match the brightness or temperature of the rooms they are placed in. "This is highly important for the owner of the plant in order for them to derive maximum satisfaction as the plant grows."

The hot list

The plants below illustrate ten of the top-performing plants in the NASA experiment. On the following pages we will look at the best plants for sunny rooms and the best plants for shady rooms, as well as highlighting a small group of plants that have an extra-special skill.

①

ARECA PALM (*Chrysalidocarpus lutescens*) A champion when it comes to removing indoor air toxins, this graceful plant is fast growing and elegant, and well-suited to a bright living room or an open-plan space. The feathery leaf fronds have a soft yellow-green tone and grow in delicate arcs that bring a lovely sense of life and movement to a room.

LADY PALM (*Rhapis excelsa*) Another leafy powerhouse when it comes to removing toxins, the lady palm is more slow growing than other palms, so it suits smaller rooms and compact homes. It has thick, glossy leaves that provide a sturdier appearance than the more delicate areca palm, and it is very easy to maintain and therefore a good choice for first-time plant owners.

②

③

BAMBOO PALM (*Chamaedorea seifrizii*) Elegant and refined, with clusters of slim canes and feathery leaves, the bamboo palm can grow up to 6 feet (2 m) tall and so is perfect for creating a "living screen" indoors if you need to divide a large open space or want to add a soft wall of green in an urban home.

RUBBER PLANT (*Ficus elastica*) One for design purists, the clean lines and sculptural beauty of the rubber plant make it a perfect partner for clean-lined architecture. These beautiful plants can grow very tall (great for larger rooms), and they have the added benefit of being fairly hardy, so will tolerate cooler temperatures and shadier conditions than the more delicate palms.

DRACAENA 'JANET CRAIG' (*Dracaena fragrans*) Perfect for livening up a shady corner, this structural plant can grow quite tall and will last for many years if well cared for. The sturdy stems and glossy dark-green leaves have a tree-like appearance and work well in a contemporary interior.

ENGLISH IVY (*Hedera helix*) If you want to add a dash of refined glamor to your home as well as scrub the air clean, English ivy is the plant for you. This pretty trailing plant will twist and drape elegantly over shelves or tumble gracefully from a hanging planter, detoxifying the air as it goes.

MINIATURE DATE PALM (*Phoenix roebelenii*) Bring the tropics to your living room with the miniature date palm. Excellent at removing toxins, it has the look of a pineapple tree, and as such it will introduce a whisper of hot skies and warm seas to your living room, whether urban or suburban.

FICUS ALII (*Ficus binnendijkii* 'Alii') For a tall houseplant with a delicate elegance, look no further than this species of ficus. Hailing from the shores of Thailand, it will appreciate a sunny spot in a bright, airy room. In return it will quietly and efficiently whisk away indoor toxins and purify the air for you year-round.

BOSTON FERN (*Nephrolepis exaltata*) On par with English ivy, the Boston fern is a very pretty indoor plant that will lend an elegance to any shelf or tabletop you place it on. It will need a little attention—regular misting and a sunny position—but it will reward you tenfold with its excellent toxin-removal powers and decorative beauty.

PEACE LILY (*Spathiphyllum wallisii*) In at number ten is the lovely peace lily, an excellent all-purpose plant that will suit almost any style of interior, thanks to its glossy tropical foliage and tall white flower stems. This beauty will be happiest in a warm spot, but it isn't too fussy about light levels and can tolerate semi-shade if required.

The best plants for a bedroom

Did you know that the majority of houseplants release oxygen during the day but not at night? So if you want to oxygenate your bedroom while you sleep, you'll need to pick one of a small tribe of plants that go against the grain and work hard to clean the air right through the evening. The following plants are all nighttime oxygenators that are believed to stand guard over you while you snooze.

· Aloe vera (*Aloe vera*)
· Dendrobium orchids (*Dendrobium*)
· Gerbera (*Gerbera*)
· Moth orchid (*Phalaenopsis*)
· Mother-in-law's tongue (*Sansevieria trifasciata*)
· Peace lily (*Spathiphyllum wallisii*)

The best plants for shady corners

These plants will cope in darker rooms and semi-shady nooks, so use them to freshen up those spaces that get the least amount of natural daylight.

· Arrowhead vine (*Syngonium podophyllum*)
· Chinese evergreen (*Aglaonema*)
· Golden pothos (*Epipremnum aureum*)
· Heartleaf philodendron (*Philodendron scandens*)
· King of hearts (*Homalomena wallisii*)
· Mother-in-law's tongue (*Sansevieria trifasciata*)
· Red emerald philodendron (*Philodendron erubescens* 'Red Emerald')
· Spadeleaf philodendron (*Philodendron domesticum*)

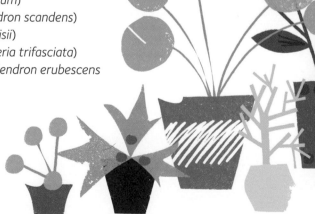

The best plants for sunny rooms

The following plants will be happy in sunny conditions (although be wary of harsh, direct sunlight), so fill a bright, warm room with a selection from this list and watch them thrive.

- Aloe vera (*Aloe vera*)
- Croton (*Codiaeum*)
- Dwarf banana (*Musa oriana*)
- Ficus alii (*Ficus binnendijkii* 'Alii')
- Florist's mum (*Chrysanthemum*)
- Gerbera daisy (*Gerbera jamesonii*)
- Kalanchoe (*Kalanchoe*)
- Norfolk Island pine (*Araucaria heterophylla*)
- Tulip (*Tulipa*)
- Wax begonia (*Begonia semperflorens*)
- Weeping fig (*Ficus benjamina*)

"The best way to detox indoor air is simply to bring in some hard-working houseplants."

Ten Ways to Decorate with Plants

If there's one thing that illustrates how fashions move in cycles, it's the current craze for houseplants. The last time they were in vogue it was the 1970s and the chicest homes were filled with woven macramé planters and large terracotta pots housing leggy spider plants and verdant ferns. But as times changed they fell out of fashion, making way for the more minimal aesthetic of the 1990s. Now, several decades later, homeowners are once again waking up to the beauty of indoor plants and I, for one, am thrilled. Here are a few ways to embrace the houseplant revival and bring a little leafy drama to your living space.

 Group them
There is something to be said for the power of an arrangement of plants. Instead of placing one lonely little plant on a shelf, try clustering pots together for maximum impact. Choose different-sized planters to vary the height, and mix various types of foliage until you hit on a combination that pleases you. Odd numbers always work better than even ones, so try a vignette of three or five plants.

2 **Dot them along bookshelves**
To add life, color, and interest to a shelf, alternate stacks of books with potted plants for a living, breathing display. Choose a plant that suits your interior and have fun with it. For example, trailing varieties, such as English ivy (*Hedera helix*), will bring a sense of grandeur to a bookcase. Or, if you want to showcase a colorful paperback collection, distribute smaller houseplants along the bookcase in vivid, colored pots to match the bright book spines.

3 **Hang them from a shower rail**
Adding plants to a bathroom can create a fun, tropical feel, but space is often limited so you will need to get creative. Try utilizing the shower rail, if you have one; just pop a couple of hanging planters over the rail and fill them with moisture-loving plants. I like to loop a small bunch of eucalyptus stems over my shower rail; the steam from the shower releases the eucalyptus oil into the air and creates a lovely scent that makes me feel like I am in a posh spa. Try it—it is surprisingly effective.

Create a jungle

Growing up, I loved the giant Swiss cheese plant (*Monstera deliciosa*) in my parents' living room. It lent a wonderful jungle-like feel to the room and seemed terribly glamorous to my younger self. If you also like the idea of creating a luscious indoor jungle, go for volume and layer up a mix of foliage-heavy specimens. Stack them at varying heights to create real impact—a plant ladder is perfect because it allows you to stagger the plants. Garden centers often stock plant ladders for outdoor use, and you can easily prop one against a wall in a living room and load it up. Alternatively, try placing a collection of plants on a cluster of small tables of different heights.

Add elegance with an orchid

For a refined interior, nothing beats the beauty of a single, tall orchid. Whether you choose an individual stem and place it by the bed or group a few together for a pretty cluster, the tall stems, delicate petals, and rich, glossy leaves will add a touch of class and instantly elevate any room in the home. I like to think of the orchid as the Grace Kelly of the plant world.

6 Suspend them

If space is at a premium, hanging planters are great for adding greenery to a small room. Add impact with one large plant, or group smaller varieties in clusters of three. Lightweight macramé planters are good for hanging near a window, as they won't obstruct the light too much, and they will also bring a touch of 1970s style to your living room. Alternatively, to liven up a plain wall or a dark corner, try a mix of brightly colored hanging planters suspended at varying heights.

7 Climb the walls

Wall-mounted plant holders can look surprisingly fresh if you choose a contemporary geometric shape or a metallic finish. They are best suited to trailing plants and varieties that don't need much water, so choose low-maintenance species and encourage them to tumble elegantly from the planter and down the wall.

"If you like the idea of creating a luscious indoor jungle, the key is to go for volume and layer up a mix of foliage-heavy specimens."

8 Fill a terrarium

A glass terrarium brimming with plants is a fun way to display greenery while keeping plants neatly enclosed. A vintage-style container will add character to a room, whereas a modern one will be right at home in a sleek urban apartment. Good for containing any mess, and easy to water and look after, terrariums are also a great way to introduce kids to caring for plants, as they can create endless tiny worlds using small succulents or miniature houseplants.

9 Create a table centerpiece

Try potted plants as a dining-table centerpiece for a leafy alternative to cut flowers. Run a series of planters down the middle of the table for impact, and dot tealights or tall candles among them for a romantic feel. For a special dinner party you could even place a tiny potted plant at each place setting as a take-home gift for your guests. I borrowed this idea from a friend, who gave each guest at her wedding a little succulent in a gold pot—a much better alternative to the usual bag of sugared almonds.

"Houseplants are an easy way to connect your indoor and outdoor spaces, as they can create a pleasing visual link to any green space you have outside your home."

Blur the boundaries

Houseplants are an easy way to connect your indoor and outdoor spaces, as they create a pleasing visual link to any green space you have outside your home. If you place a few floor-standing houseplants near any outdoor access points, such as patio doors or balcony windows, you will start to blur the boundaries between indoors and out. I tried this in my little guest bedroom, which had the potential to be a bit of a wasted space because it serves as a walk-through from the house to the backyard. Placing plants on both sides of the patio doors immediately gave the room a fresh lease on life and transformed it into a leafy extension of the garden.

And finally ...
TAKE CARE

If you have children or pets at home, be aware that some houseplants can be poisonous, so do double-check before you introduce them to your living spaces. Babies and toddlers are especially at risk, since they have a habit of trying to eat anything and everything they can get their hands on, so it is very important to ensure that any plants you place within potential reach of little fingers are nontoxic if ingested.

- Place plants out of reach of small hands and pets
- Cover pebbles or soil with mesh to prevent ingestion
- Choose nontoxic plants

How to Decorate with the Happiest Color

If you had to choose the happiest color, which shade would you go for? Sky blue, maybe? Ruby red? Or how about sunshine yellow? Colors can be very emotive, and I bet you already use them, without realizing, to describe your emotions or state of mind. If you have ever described yourself as "feeling blue" or being "green with envy," for example, then you have already formed a link between color and mood. But would it surprise you to learn that experts think they have discovered a universal "happiest color"?

According to research undertaken by a team at the University of Manchester, when it comes to colors that make us feel happy, there is a clear winner. And on the flipside, there is also an official "unhappy" color. Read on to see if you agree.

Bring Me Sunshine

So, what are these happy and unhappy colors? According to this research, the happiest color is . . . yellow. And the unhappiest color is . . . gray.

That sounds about right, doesn't it? The happiest color brings to mind images of sunshine and warmth, while the unhappiest color is redolent of rain clouds and chilly weather. But can it really be that clear-cut? And just how did researchers test this theory?

The discovery was the result of research undertaken by Professor Peter Whorwell and Dr. Helen Carruthers, who sought to establish a link between colors and mood. They created a color wheel using thirty-eight colors, including black, white, and shades of gray, and then divided their test subjects into two groups: those who identified as anxious and/or depressed and those who did not. They then asked each person three questions: which color represented their mood, which was their favorite, and which they were drawn to.

The most popular favorite, chosen by everyone, across the board, was blue. But, and this is where it gets interesting: When subjects were asked which color they felt most drawn to, both sets of participants mostly chose yellow. And when asked which color represented their mood, yellow was most often chosen by non-depressed or -anxious people, while gray was the more common choice for the other group. These findings led the researchers to conclude that yellow was most often linked with a happy mood and gray with an unhappy mood.

I asked Joa Studholme, International Color Consultant for the paint company Farrow & Ball, what she makes of this research. "I am a huge advocate of color having mood-enriching properties," she says. "It's a powerful medium that has an effect at both a conscious and a subconscious level." But while she agrees that strong yellows are "certainly stimulating and engender a lively mood," she cautions against jumping right in and decorating with too much strong yellow, instead advising a less-is-more approach to avoid the risk of the shade looking too garish.

With this in mind, I have pulled together some mood-boosting decorating tips to help you infuse your home with the happiest hue.

Here Comes the Sun
How to Decorate with Yellow

Small changes have a big impact with this sunny shade, so dip a toe in the water with one of these easy decorating updates and bring a little sunshine indoors.

Cast a warm light

A classic decorating trick for bringing a soft glow to a room is to line the inside of a lampshade with a heat-resistant fabric in a warm yellow tone or to choose a lampshade with a burnished gold interior. Try this in rooms where you want to create warmth and evoke a soft, diffused atmosphere, such as a bedroom or a living room. You can also try hanging a yellow-lined pendant light low over a dining table to bathe your guests (and you) in a warm pool of flattering golden light.

Choosing yellow-toned lightbulbs is another instant and budget-friendly way to warm up the atmosphere of a room. If you have ever looked into the window of a bright, inviting living room from the outside on a dark evening, you already know the appeal of warm, yellow-hued light. Opening up the front door to be greeted by a glow of golden light spilling out across the front step is a very welcoming sight to return home to.

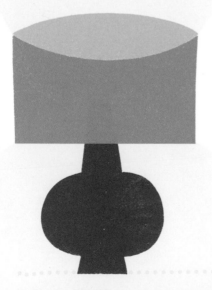

"A glow of yellow light spilling out across the front step is a very welcoming sight to return home to."

Welcome guests

One of the places you can afford to be bold is in an area that is just used as a transitional space, from outside to in. Try adding a splash of yellow to an entryway or hallway for a mood-enhancing lift every time you pass through. "A vibrant yellow hall is always welcoming," says Joa, so try bringing in a little sunshine with your décor choices. It doesn't have to be a big change; I have an egg-yolk-yellow vase near my front door that lifts my mood every time I see it, especially when it is filled with a delightful bunch of garden flowers. Hanging art with yellow tones or using a bright yellow lampshade would have the same effect. Or, if you are feeling bold, dive right in and paint your walls a cheerful buttercup yellow to add energy and zest to a hallway.

Mimic a sunny day

Joa suggests using yellow on windows "to create a sense of sunshine," and there are several ways to do this in your own home. Painting the inside trim of your windows is a great styling tip for mimicking the effect of warm sunshine, and you don't have to choose a strong shade for this—even a soft wash of primrose yellow would have a cheering effect. Alternatively, you could hang a brightly colored window blind or shade with yellow tones woven through the pattern to bring a sense of summer into your home all year round.

Show your sunny side

Yellow is a wonderful highlight color, and it works well to draw attention to a piece of statement furniture. Treating a piece of vintage furniture to a coat of yellow paint is a great way to give it a new lease on life. To create a statement on a budget, try giving an old wooden chair a coat of creamy yellow paint and mixing it in with other chairs around a dining table. Or, for a more subtle flash of sunshine, update a country-style wooden dining table by painting the legs yellow to contrast with the warm grain of the wooden tabletop.

Walking on sunshine

Dark floors can be quickly and easily updated with a cheerful rug, so if you want to add a burst of sunshine yellow underfoot, choose a brightly patterned rug and you will have happy feet every time you walk across it. Geometric patterns are a great partner for strong yellow shades and a peppy yellow-and-white patterned rug will instantly brighten up a gloomy hallway or add a fun touch to a children's playroom. Choose a hard-wearing or weatherproof rug and you can even add some yellow underfoot outdoors, too.

Try golden touches

Textiles are a quick and inexpensive way to change the look and feel of a room, so if you want to experiment with yellow but aren't sure about making a permanent commitment, test the waters with a buttercup-colored throw or a decorative pillow in sunshine yellow. Mix in one or two yellow throw pillows with other uplifting shades on a sofa to create a look you love, or try a soft wool throw across the foot of a bed to warm up a bedroom. Think about textures, too; velvet is a contemporary choice for accent pillows and one in mustard yellow can look elegant and smart when placed against a gray or navy sofa.

Hang happy artwork

Changing your artwork is a great way to introduce color to a room without the permanence of other design options. Don't be intimidated by choosing and buying art; the secret to deciding on any kind of décor for your home is just to ask yourself if you really love it—don't worry about what others will think or if it's a "good investment." If it cheers you each time you look at it, then it's money well spent, whether it's an original oil painting or a cheap and cheerful poster. If you are on a budget, there are still plenty of affordable ways to brighten up your walls. In my home office I have tacked up a display of postcards above the desk with yellow washi tape, and I update them whenever the mood strikes me. You could also frame your favorite magazine covers, or paint picture frames a zesty citrus shade to bathe your photos in sunshine.

> *"The secret to deciding on any kind of décor for your home is just to ask yourself if you really love it—don't worry about what others will think."*

Look to nature

First impressions count, so if you want to feel happy each time you open your front door, plant colorful flowerpots with bold yellow flowers and group them directly outside the entrance to your home. A climbing honeysuckle (*Lonicera*) or a rambling jasmine (*Jasminum*) would look wonderful around a front door if you have the space, or try a terracotta pot crammed with daffodils (*Narcissus*) in springtime. You could also plant sunflowers (*Helianthus*), primroses (*Primula*), tulips (*Tulipa*), roses (*Rosa*), magnolia (*Magnolia*), or any other yellow-toned flower that strikes your fancy. Alternatively, you could choose (or paint) a sunny yellow plant pot and fill it with a mix of vibrant blooms to brighten up a porch or front step. Don't have any outside space? Try a hanging basket or window box instead.

When life gives you lemons

Lemon trees are surprisingly easy to look after, and the scent and sight of fresh, zingy lemons are mood-boosting tonics in themselves. I have a small lemon tree in a terracotta pot that I keep sheltered in the winter and then move to a sunny spot as soon as the weather warms up. I bought it after a trip to the Amalfi coast in Italy, where lemon trees line the streets and their fresh, summery scent perfumes the air. Small citrus trees can have a long fruiting season if you look after them carefully, and I can't recommend them enough; the joy you will get from seeing each new yellow fruit peeking out from underneath the waxy green leaves is a great reward for your efforts. As well as these little droplets of yellow treasure, my tree also provides the prettiest snow-white blossom, the scent of which is like bottled sunshine and instantly transports me back to the sparkling seas and sunny beaches of Capri.

Create Your Own Sunshine
How to Make Yellow Work Whatever Your Style

There is a yellow out there for everyone, and the tone you choose can have a huge impact on the mood you create. "Rooms can be made to feel more formal or relaxed with the use of color," agrees Joa. "Colder colors [are] more formal and warmer colors more relaxed. Small rooms can become flamboyant with strong color, and large rooms become airy by lack of color."

Make it traditional

If bright lemon yellow isn't the shade for you, try introducing mellower, warmer caramel tones, and mixing them in with buttery neutrals for a softer look in a traditional-style interior. These quieter tones would sit more comfortably with dark wood furniture and classic décor, and, in this setting, soft yellow can be used as a neutral. Layer up different tones to add interest, bring in plenty of texture, and contrast it with crisp white for an elegant feel.

Take it to the country

Yellow can also look surprisingly at home in a country-style interior. Try bringing in elements of rich, egg-yolk yellow and contrast them with pretty, bright florals and/or soft stripes. Keep the finish matte for a casual look. A country-style hutch, for example, would look wonderful painted a rich, warm yellow and filled with a selection of mismatched crockery, cheerful table linens, and a container of garden flowers.

Be bright and beautiful

Yellow is a powerful shade, so it can have a real impact in a contemporary home. Add a playful touch by introducing a flash of zesty color where it is going to be least expected, such as the lining of a curtain or around a doorframe. Painting the inside edge of a door is another way to defy convention and reveal a small sliver of sunshine each time you open it. Just be sure to use this accent color sparingly—to highlight small details, add drama, or introduce an element of fun.

Find Your Own Happy

While yellow seems to be the winner for the happiest color, at least according to the experiment carried out by Professor Whorwell and Dr. Carruthers, there were several other colors on the wheel that had positive connotations, and the truth is that everyone sees color differently. While you might want to use yellow in some rooms to create an uplifting mood, other areas of the home might call for different moods—and therefore different colors. "Most people want to create either a sense of calm or a feeling of intimacy," agrees Joa. "The magic of color is that you can do this with ease."

So if yellow isn't the shade for you, or if you want to use color to create different moods in different areas of your home, take a look at the chart below and discover your own happy shades.

1 **Pick your mood**
Look at the color chart and write down how each color makes you feel: happy, sad, calm, energized, etc.

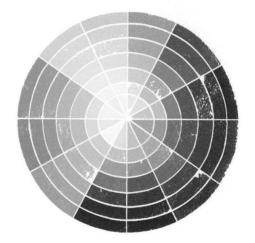

2 **List your rooms**
Now write down how you want to feel in each room of your home: living room, kitchen, bedroom, bathroom, office, and children's room(s).

3 **You've got a match!**
Now match up your moods and rooms. For example, if you decided that soft blue made you feel the most relaxed and calm, and you also identified that you want your bedroom to make you feel this way, then you've got a match. Get everyone in your home to do the same exercise, and you will start to build up a color-mood map that you can use to decorate your home.

Things You Need to Know Before You Start Decorating

I asked Joa for tips to help you get started with adding color to your rooms. "The joy of decorating with color is that there are no rules!" she says. "It is the best way to express one's individuality." That said, she also always advises people to think about the following three things before they start:

1 **Consider the light in the room**
"Embrace it, don't fight it, which often means painting darker spaces in stronger, darker colors and light spaces in light, airy colors."

2 **Think about more than just the color on the walls**
"You need to make choices about the woodwork, ceiling, and any bits of joinery or painted furniture, too. They are all like small ingredients in a recipe, which need to be perfectly balanced within the room."

3 **Always choose colors that you feel comfortable with**
"You don't need to use colors that are historically correct for your architecture, and you certainly don't have to use gray just because everyone else is!"

And finally . . .

While gray didn't win any prizes in the happy-color contest, this versatile shade still has a lot going for it, and it has enjoyed a huge surge in popularity recently. I asked Joa to offer some tips on using gray to create a good mood in the home.

"Gray has been, without doubt, the most fashionable color to use in the home for the past five years, and it certainly does not create an unhappy atmosphere. However, you need to take care to use warmer grays, especially in north light (in the northern hemisphere), since cold grays can feel too gritty and industrial for most homes. Lighter gray on the walls with a slightly darker gray on the woodwork will create a space that remains light and airy but has a feeling of sophistication."

3

Tidy Your Way to Happiness

Can a tidy home make you healthier and happier? According to research, yes, it can. Darby E. Saxbe and Rena Repetti, researchers at UCLA, discovered that women who described their living spaces as cluttered or full of unfinished projects were more likely to be depressed and fatigued than women who described their homes as restful and restorative.

It sounds obvious, doesn't it? A tidy home makes us happy, and a messy one makes us unhappy. The researchers also found that women with cluttered homes produced higher levels of the stress hormone cortisol, and you know that can't be good. But can you reverse this trend and clean your way to happiness and health? Absolutely! According to a study in the *British Journal of Sports Medicine*, cleaning your home vigorously for twenty minutes nonstop once a week can improve levels of anxiety, distress, or depression. So if you want to grab some of those health benefits for yourself, it's time to wave goodbye to stressful clutter and say hello to a tidy, streamlined home. This chapter will show you how.

Six Daily Habits of Tidy People

If you like the idea of a tidy home but clutter seems to just build up at every turn, don't worry, you are not alone. But there is a way to fake it until you make it. Here are six habits to borrow from tidy people. (I borrowed them from my sister.)

Just do it

Waiting for the perfect moment to declutter your home? Here's the secret: That moment is now. Tidy people like my sister don't leave jobs until later, they pick up clutter as soon as they see it, they wash their dishes when they have finished eating, and they make the bed as soon as they hop out of it. Yes, those people really do exist, and yes, you can become one, too, with a little practice.

Make a list

If chores seem insurmountable, break them down into bite-sized chunks and work through them methodically. Messy people see clutter as an unscalable mountain. Tidy people see it as a series of walks up gentle hills.

Find a place for everything

Tidy people don't have piles of assorted items all over their home because *they have a dedicated space for everything.* If I finish reading a magazine at my sister's house, I'll leave it on the table and minutes later it's whisked away into the magazine rack; if I put my phone on the kitchen counter, it's moved to the charging dock in the hallway. I've implemented a version of this (admittedly, a more relaxed version) in my own home and it really does work.

4 Tidy as you go

Cooking a meal? Tidy people will clean up as they go, rather than leave a pile of pots and pans and dirty chopping boards for later. The same applies to a craft or DIY project; if you get out a stack of art materials or a pot of paint and a paintbrush, put them away as soon as you finish with them, rather than leaving a mess to deal with later. Think of it as short-term pain, long-term gain. The happiness of finishing a meal and knowing there is no dishwashing to be done is not to be underestimated.

5 Make your bed

Tidy people know that just pulling the bedding up and fluffing the pillows immediately after getting out of bed makes the bedroom look instantly tidy and organized and starts your day off on the right foot. I've begun doing it, and it's incredibly good for giving you a proud little glow first thing in the morning. Plus it only takes thirty seconds, so everyone has time for that. Do it.

6 Edit down

Do you need two of those? Really? Tidy people will ruthlessly edit the items in their home on a regular basis. They don't need to have a huge decluttering session because they don't let items build up in the first place. Cast a similarly critical eye over your home and start to filter out unnecessary items on a daily basis. Cupboard full of kitchen appliances you've only used once? Sell or donate them. Old coats cluttering up your hall closet? Donate them to a charity and reclaim your storage space.

Five Things to Get Rid of Today

 Clothes that don't fit or flatter
Trust me, if you haven't worn an item of clothing in the past year, you are not likely to wear it in the next twelve months. Clothes need to make you feel amazing, so anything that doesn't make you feel great, flatter your figure, or work hard for its keep is out. A common tip for implementing this rule is to turn all your clothes hangers the wrong way on the rack, and then as you wear something, turn the hanger the right way around. Any hangers that haven't been turned around within a year indicate that the item needs to go. It works.

 **Old college notes or memorabilia**
Yes, you put a lot of work into your university degree, but what are you keeping all your old research notes for? Are you planning to review them all one day? Or perhaps you might invite all your friends and family over one evening and read sections aloud to them? If the honest answer is no (and I hope it is), then it's time to let them go. The same goes for old tickets, catalogs, or brochures that you kept for sentimental value. Allow yourself to keep a few items that really mean a lot to you and store them neatly in a box, then recycle everything else.

3 Old phones, chargers, and tech items

Keeping tech "just in case" is a surefire way to acquire a drawer full of items you won't use. Don't do it. Take any old phones, tablets, or computers to recycling centers or trade them in for money off your next purchase.

4 Old kitchen gadgets

If it's broken, gathering dust, or hasn't been used in the past two years, it's time to recycle or donate it. Yes, that means the bread maker, the ice-cream maker, and the mountains of old mismatched plastic storage containers. Once you've cut the apron strings and gotten rid of all those items you've been hoarding "just in case," you will instantly free up valuable kitchen cupboard space.

5 Old paperwork

As a guide, keep one year's worth of bills and paperwork and seven years' worth of tax records, then shred the rest, but do check first with your tax advisor to find out exactly what you need to keep. If you work freelance you may need to keep several years' worth of paperwork for tax reasons.

NOTE
Old electrical items need to be disposed of properly, usually at a recycling center.

Five Clutter Hotspots
and How to Banish Them

Bedside tables

In theory, your bedside table would be home to a single thought-provoking novel, an elegant reading lamp, and a glass for water; in reality, it's probably piled up with an awful lot more than that. Because bedrooms have limited work surfaces, bedside tables are magnets for clutter. Here's how to impose a sense of order and calm.

Edit ruthlessly

Visual clutter, especially the kind that reminds you of things you need to do, is really unhelpful when you are trying to drift off to sleep. So ask yourself what you actually need by your bed, and edit accordingly. I tried this in my own bedroom and ended up removing seven unread books, two magazines, three pairs of earrings, two pairs of sunglasses, several hairbands, and a hairbrush. The only items I kept were a reading lamp, one book, and a tray for my jewelry. If you find your bedside table magically accumulates clutter, like mine did, try a similar edit and be ruthless.

Create a "pocket tray"

Think about your bedtime routine. If you tend to remove your jewelry or empty your pockets when getting ready for bed, find a tray or storage box to corral all of those small items and keep them tidy. Loose change, cufflinks, earrings, and keys are all common clutter culprits, so assign them a box and sweep them into it every evening. This can be one of the items you allow yourself to keep on your bedside table.

Choose a table with storage

Even if you have the best intentions, clutter will accumulate, so preempt it by choosing a bedside table with storage drawers or baskets, then do a once-over every night and put anything nonessential into a drawer or stash it in a basket and tuck it away under the table.

Bathroom countertops

Perfume bottles, toothpaste tubes, empty shampoo bottles—clutter can build up at a mystifyingly rapid rate in a bathroom when several members of the family are using it. These quick tips will help to restore order.

Divide and conquer

Impose order by allocating each member of the family their own drawer or container and keeping only a few items out on the countertop. If you don't have enough storage space for everyone to have a drawer, decorative boxes or lidded wicker baskets are good alternatives. Gather all nonessential items into these containers after use and pop the lid on to regain some order. A colorful plastic box with holes for drainage for corralling children's bath toys is also a good idea if you want to limit the bathtime chaos and avoid stepping on a hard plastic toy with bare feet (ouch!).

Group essentials

For items that are used every day and need to be kept out on the countertop, such as hand soap, hand lotion, and toothbrushes, group them all together on a tray and keep them close to the sink to avoid splashing water all over the countertop when you reach for them. Choose beautiful bottles or containers that you will be happy to look at every day, too; I decant my liquid hand soap into a glass dispenser because I'd rather look at that than a plastic bottle, but whatever pleases your eye is the right choice for you.

Tidy towels

Large storage boxes are good for keeping clean towels neatly ordered, and plenty of wall hooks will ensure wet towels don't end up on the floor. Color-coded towels are useful if you have lots of people using a bathroom—and culprits can be easily identified when damp towels are left lying around. If your towels are all the same, a simple colored tab or marker dot on the label can help you assign each one to a family member. If you are really organized, why not take a page from my sister's book and embroider each person's name onto their own set of towels? Instant identification!

That kitchen drawer

You know the one—the drawer that's stuffed with takeout menus, batteries, scissors, pens, paperclips, old receipts, and who knows what else. We all have one of these offenders and, actually, we all need one; where else would you stash all those random items that don't belong anywhere else? That said, the best way to keep on top of it all is to regularly dive in and sort through it.

Take stock

Clear everything out of the drawer and group like items with like items. Roll up lengths of string neatly, stack menus in a pile, and sort through all those single batteries to see which are charged and which need to be recycled. If there is a more logical place to store something, find it a new home. If there really isn't anywhere else for it to live, it can go back in the drawer. But be scrupulous.

Buy a dividing tray

Find a tray or dividing system for the drawer (a flatware tray is good for this) and designate a space for each of the different groups of items. Now fill it up section by section. Place all of the items you need to access daily (pens, scissors, string) at the front, and move those that are used less often (batteries, menus, birthday candles) to the back.

Banish layers

The tipping point for a messy drawer is usually when several items get layered on top of each other, because as soon as you start having to sift around to find what you need, looking under papers and behind rolls of string, any system that you have in place quickly unravels. So be strict with yourself and don't put anything on top of your newly ordered storage system. If an item doesn't fit into a compartment, it doesn't go in the drawer.

The entryway floor

Your entryway will need to work extra hard to stay tidy with the amount of daily traffic it has to deal with and the number of items that need to be accessed every day. If you find yourself tripping over shoes, umbrellas, or children's toys the second you walk through the door, it could be time for a blitz. Here's how to transform your entryway from cluttered to calm.

Storage, storage, storage

I am obsessed with storage and don't think you can ever have too much. Entryway storage, in particular, can be really appealing; wall hooks, mail trays, umbrella stands, and storage benches can totally transform a messy entryway and provide a great opportunity to stamp your personality on your home.

Floor space is usually limited, so start with the walls. Peg racks are great for a country-style foyer and can be run along the length of your wall for maximum coat storage, or choose brightly colored hooks for a cheerful welcome in a contemporary space. Hooks labeled with names are good for allocating each member of the family a designated space to hang their coat, and high shelves are good for stashing away items that aren't needed every day.

Be seasonal

In the height of summer do you need to have wet-weather gear cluttering up the entryway? And, equally, do you need to take up valuable storage space with sandals and beach bags in the winter? Do a seasonal review of your entryway closets and remove any items that aren't required. Store them somewhere else, such as under a guest bed or in the attic, until they are needed again, swapping out seasons as necessary.

Squeeze in a slim table

Having a place for keys, mail, and your phone is essential in a entryway if you want to avoid dropping them on various tables around the house. If you have enough space to squeeze in a slim console table, it will definitely pull its weight. The secret to blissful order is to place a few trays or dishes on top and designate one for each item that you tend to put down when you walk through the door.

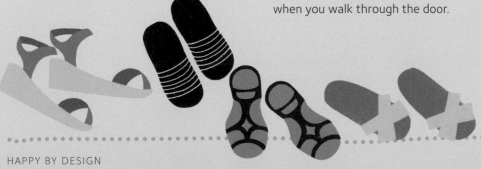

Kitchen countertops

The kitchen is another hard-working space that gets a lot of daily traffic, and kitchen counters and islands in particular can accumulate clutter at an alarming speed. I find that stray pieces of paperwork, such as unpaid bills and receipts, mysteriously migrate to my kitchen countertop—I have no idea how—along with a motley selection of items "on their way to somewhere else." Here are a few tips to keep surfaces clean and tidy.

Have an inbox

If letters, bills, and homework tend to migrate to your kitchen counters, set up a box or tray to keep these things tidy and together. A slim tray is better, as a large box will only encourage paperwork to build up, making the problem worse. Use it as an active inbox, to be sorted through daily, and it will keep everything in one place and prevent individual letters and bills from drifting across the countertop.

Maximize wall storage

Clutter attracts more clutter, so clearing your countertops of anything that is nonessential will allow you a clean slate from which to start. Many items that clutter up kitchen counters can usually be hung on the wall with a little creative thought. Try hanging utensils from a bar or a series of hooks, storing spices and herbs on a wall-mounted rack, and placing vegetables in wall-hung wire containers.

Limit food containers on countertops

It's nice to have a few everyday essentials out on the counter, such as a bowl of fruit, but when food containers start to take over, it's time to be ruthless. Store most food items in cupboards or out of sight, choosing just one or two items that you like to display or see every day.

4

Unlock the Secret to a Good Night's Sleep

When was the last time you had a really good night's sleep? I mean the kind of deep, refreshing sleep that enables you to spring out of bed the next morning, full of optimism and energy for the day ahead? If you can't remember the last occasion, then it could be time to overhaul your sleeping habits and start to take your rest time seriously—because a good sleep routine is one of the most crucial elements to get right if you want to boost your health, well-being, and happiness levels at home.

Can a Good Night's Sleep Make Us Happier?

No one doubts the mood-boosting magic of a good night's sleep, but I wanted to find out just why so many of us struggle to get enough of it and what happens to our bodies when we don't hit our nightly quota. I set out to discover if and how we can reverse negative sleep patterns. Follow along as I unearth some easy steps we can all take to improve our sleep at home and attain that magical eight hours of refreshing slumber each and every night.

For some tips about all things relaxing, I quizzed Lisa Artis, spokesperson for the Sleep Council, a UK organization that promotes healthy sleep. "Just one bad night's sleep affects our mood, concentration, and alertness," she says, "while long-term sleep deprivation has far more serious consequences: It's been linked to a number of serious health problems, such as high blood pressure, heart disease, diabetes, and stroke." But before you panic your way to another sleepless night, Lisa is also a huge advocate of the positive impact of a good night's sleep on health and happiness levels, and she has some practical advice about how we can all reset our bad habits.

So if we overhaul our sleeping habits and routines, can this make us happier? "It certainly can!" says Lisa. "As with proper nutrition and exercise, sleep fulfills a vital role in keeping us healthy and happy. We need a good night's sleep to ensure we're feeling fit, thinking sharply, and generally having the appetite and enthusiasm to make the most of everyday living."

"A good sleep routine is one of the most crucial elements to get right if you want to boost your health, well-being, and happiness levels at home."

The Action Plan

The best place to start when undoing bad sleep habits and resetting your nighttime routine is, naturally, your bedroom. There are a few common mistakes that we are all guilty of—reading your phone in bed, anyone?—so I asked Lisa what the top offenders are when it comes to disturbed sleep. On the following pages I will show you quick and easy ways to fix these problems.

Four things that may be ruining your sleep . . .

1 **Daylight**
Getting the light levels right in your bedroom can have a big impact on sleep, as too much light can hamper your ability to get your nightly Zs. "A dark room is most conducive to sleep, as light tells your body it's time to wake up," explains Lisa. "In darkness, your body releases a hormone called melatonin that relaxes your body, helping you to drift off." (See also page 95.)

2 **Heat**
Do you struggle to fall asleep in the summer months? If your bedroom is too hot, it could be preventing you from getting good-quality sleep. "Ideally, bedrooms should be around 60 to 65°F [15–18°C]," says Lisa. "Your body temperature needs to lower slightly before you go to sleep, which is why it's difficult to drop off when you're too hot."

3 **Tech**
Do you go to bed at a sensible hour, full of good intentions to make it an early night, only to then spend an hour aimlessly scrolling through your social media accounts, shopping online, and watching videos of cats? If so, you are not alone, but it could be time to cut the habit. "All this nonstop stimulation causes havoc when we're trying to fall asleep," says Lisa. "Switch off your tech at least an hour before bedtime, and that includes your phone."

4 **Colors**
What color is your bedroom? If it is a strong or bright shade, it could be time to get out the paint and paintbrush. "Strong colors can stimulate your energy, resulting in poor sleep," warns Lisa. "Conversely, pastels and calming shades promote a more relaxing environment." (See pages 34 and 35 for more information on mood and color.)

. . . and How to Fix Them

Now we know what is preventing us from falling asleep, but what can we do about it? The following advice will help you to create a snug, cozy, and cool bedroom that will allow you to drift effortlessly into a peaceful night's sleep, no sheep counting required.

Block the light

Make sure your curtains are long enough

Drapes that stop too short or end at windowsill height will usually let in slivers of light around the edges, so if you can, invest in curtains that sweep right down to the floor and help block any light from sneaking into the room. I love the luxurious effect of curtains gently pooling onto the floor, but if that isn't your thing—and it does divide opinion—just ensure that your drapes lightly brush the floor instead. Make sure they don't hover shy of the carpet because, as well as allowing light to sneak in, this also has the unfortunate effect of making them look like a pair of trousers that are too short.

Use blackout fabric

Blackout fabric is your secret weapon in the fight against daylight and is particularly invaluable in a child's bedroom if you need to darken the space for midday naps or early bedtimes. Drapes can be backed or interlined with blackout fabric for really good light protection, and blinds can be made in blackout fabric, too. If you use both blackout blinds and blackout curtains, you really will create a hibernation-worthy den.

Double up

If you want to really lightproof your room, you will need to layer up your window treatments. I have a light-colored blackout blind installed within the window frame of my bedroom window, as well as heavy linen curtains in front, and the two of these combined ensure the room is dark, tranquil, and restful when it needs to be. Double window treatments are also a great way to play with pattern in a bedroom; a patterned Roman shade hung behind plain curtains will add a shot of color and interest during the day and can be tucked out of sight behind neutral curtains at night.

Play it cool

Go natural

To keep your body temperature at a comfortable level during the night, choose cotton or linen sheets over synthetic materials; the same goes for anything you wear in bed. Natural materials will allow your skin to breathe and will help wick away moisture and regulate your temperature throughout the night. Investing in an all-season duvet is a good option for temperature regulation, too; they are usually made of two lightweight duvets that can be used individually in the summer months and then fastened together to create a heavyweight layer for winter.

Create a cool breeze

Even with the right bedding, trying to get to sleep on hot summer nights can be a struggle if your room isn't properly ventilated, so it is important to try to keep your bedroom as cool as possible, even during the day. In hot weather, keep the windows open and the curtains drawn during the day to keep the temperature low, and use a fan if you need to bring the temperature down further before you go to sleep. During the heatwave in summer 2017, when it seemed that the entire world was struggling to sleep, a friend shared a great tip with me for creating instant (and cheap) air-conditioning: Place a bowl of iced water in front of a tabletop fan, angled so that the air from the fan skims across the ice, and you

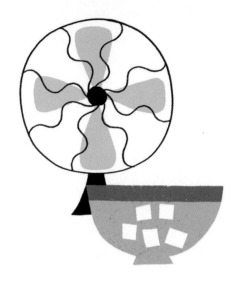

get a deliciously cool stream of "iced air." It really does work, and it's a great trick to try on days when the air is stiflingly hot.

Make a cold-water bottle

Hot-water bottles are usually associated with chilly evenings and brisk winter nights, for obvious reasons, but on a very warm summer's night, try filling your hot-water bottle with cold water and pop it in the freezer for a few hours to create an iced-water bottle. Pop it under the covers an hour or so before bedtime so that when you climb into bed it will be deliciously cool.

> *"An hour spent browsing social media accounts on your phone before bed could tell your mind that you are not ready for sleep, while your exhausted body is trying to tell you that you are."*

Turn off tech

Minimize blue light

Are you feeling "tired but wired"? Too much blue light from digital devices at night can be seriously detrimental to your sleep patterns, as it interferes with the body's production of melatonin, which can lead to the effect of being physically tired but mentally alert. For example, an hour spent browsing social media accounts on your phone before bed could tell your mind that you are not ready for sleep, while your exhausted body is trying to tell you that you are. To get back on track, try limiting your use of phones and tablets before bed or, if you really can't face doing that, switch the screen to nighttime mode to reduce the levels of blue light (see page 154).

Banish LED displays

Bright LED displays on alarm clocks can be a distracting light source when you are trying to doze, plus having a visual reminder of the time when you are desperately trying to get to sleep is never helpful. Choose an analog clock instead, or one without a backlit display, to get rid of any unnecessary light in the bedroom.

Switch off the TV

TVs in bedrooms are a tricky topic. Many people have them and, yes, they are convenient for watching a movie before you go to sleep, but they can dominate the one room that is supposed to be a calm and peaceful retreat from the rest of your home. Add to this the fact that they can also seriously hamper our ability to sleep and I am ready to ban them from the bedroom. But if you aren't ready to banish your bedroom TV, then at least make sure you switch it off well before you try to go to sleep, as the flickering screen can disrupt the production of the sleep hormone melatonin.

Relax with a tranquil palette
Paint your way to sleep

Soothing colors are essential in a bedroom, where the aim is to create a peaceful environment to help you to unwind from the day and transition into sleep. Soft tones are better than bright, energizing colors, but color is very subjective, so the trick is to choose a shade that you identify as soothing and calming (see page 34). Consider soft shades of blue, light neutrals, or gentle pastel tones.

Favor natural-toned bed linen

Your bed linen will make up a considerable proportion of the palette in your bedroom, so choose it wisely. A plain white or light-toned duvet or comforter cover is much more relaxing to look at than a busy, patterned one, which is visually stimulating and not conducive to winding down. If you do want to bring in a color, layer a patterned throw or bedspread on top of a plain cover.

Consider artwork

Soothing scenes or abstract canvases can work better in a bedroom than busy pictures or brightly colored artwork, which can be too energizing. Pick patterns or scenes that make you feel rested and soothed, or choose a type print with a calming mantra.

Elevate Your Evening Routine
Four Nightly Rituals to Help You Unwind

Now that you have set up your bedroom for optimum sleep, think about how you can carve out some time each night to mentally and physically unwind and move yourself into a more relaxed frame of mind before bed. Here are some evening relaxation routines you can adopt to ensure you are in the right head space when your head hits the pillow.

1 Write down your worries

I am really bad about allowing lots of small worries to build up into one large, looming cloud of anxiety, and these worry clouds tend to gather just when I need to drift off to sleep. If you also find yourself wide awake at 2 a.m. with an undefinable sense of anxiety, it can really help to write everything down. It will give you some perspective on exactly what is worrying you. Before you go to bed, make a note of everything that is troubling you, from the big concerns to the tiny ones, and then try to write an action point next to each item. For example, are you worried about a presentation you have to do at work? Write down the worry and then add a note to ask a colleague to help you with a run-through in the morning, for example. Writing down your worries won't instantly eliminate all your concerns, but it will turn them into more manageable items and might allow your brain a little bit of breathing space.

② Take a warm (not hot) bath

Any routine or habit that allows you to transition from a busy day to a more relaxed disposition before bedtime is a good thing. Taking a bath just before bed can really help you switch into sleep mode, and if you add a relaxing scent into the mix, such as lavender bath oil, you get extra points. But do make sure the bath water is warm, as opposed to piping hot, and avoid really strong scents; both of these things are actually detrimental to sleep.

3 Plan your next day in advance

I am always in a rush in the mornings. No matter how much I would like to be calm and organized, there always seems to be a sense of urgency—some might say drama—to my mornings. To be kind to my future self, I have started planning the next morning before I go to bed. I think about where I need to be the next day, decide what I am going to wear, and put my bag ready by the front door to try to mitigate any last-minute crises. I spend extra time doing this if I know I have a particularly busy day ahead or an important event coming up, because otherwise I will lie awake worrying about it and waste precious sleep time. If you find that you are getting anxious about the next day, or if, like me, you are just not a morning person, try to spend a few minutes before you get into bed mentally running through the day ahead and prepping in any way you can. That allows you to go to bed with an easy mind and, dare I say it, a touch of self-satisfaction, too.

4 Set a "bedtime"

If you have children, you already know the importance of routines, especially when it comes to nap times and bedtimes. Treat your own sleep in the same way and try to go to bed and wake up at around the same time each day to establish a sleep schedule. I get up for work every day at 7 a.m., so I aim to be in bed by 11 p.m., and I try to treat my weekends the same way. Admittedly, this can be difficult if you have had a busy week and want to treat yourself by sleeping in on the weekend, so don't be too hard on yourself if you don't get up at precisely the same time every day. That said, if you can stick to roughly the same schedule, regardless of weekdays or weekends, it will really help you to regulate your sleep.

And Finally . . .

How to Find Your Dream Mattress

If you've followed all the steps in this chapter so far, you've now optimized your bedroom design. You've chosen soothing colors, written down all your worries, and put technology firmly in its place. But there's still one, crucial element to get right: your bed. Choosing the right bed frame and mattress is essential in the quest for a peaceful, relaxed slumber, so I asked the researchers at the Sleep Council to shed some light on how to choose the perfect bed. They suggest asking yourself five questions (see below) about your mattress and the quality of your sleep.

Do you need a new bed?

If the answer is yes to any of the following, it is time to find yourself a new mattress.

- ☐ Have you had your mattress for more than seven years?

- ☐ Do you wake up with stiffness and/or aches and pains?

- ☐ Are you sleeping worse than you did a year ago?

- ☐ Have you had a better night's sleep in a bed other than yours?

- ☐ Does your mattress show signs of visible wear and tear (it sags, is lumpy, and so on)?

TOP TIP
Set aside enough time to do the job of mattress shopping properly. Don't shop when you are tired or rushed—you run the risk that all the beds will feel wonderful!

What size?

If you share your bed, the Sleep Council experts recommend that you should both be able to lie side by side with your arms behind your head and your elbows out, without touching. They also suggest that your bed be 4 to 6 inches (10–15 cm) longer than the tallest partner.

Take the test

A good way to check if the bed you are lying on is too soft, too hard, or just right is to lie on your back and slide your hand under the hollow of your back. If it slides in too easily, the bed may be too hard for you (leading to pressure on your hips and shoulders). If it is a struggle to slide your hand in, the bed is probably too soft. If you can move your hand with just a little resistance, the bed may be just right for you.

Sleep tight!

5

Discover the Happiest Scents

Scent can be an intensely individual thing, and fragrances are often tightly woven with memories. If you have ever experienced a rush of nostalgia when a particular perfume catches you by surprise, you will know how deeply personal our sense of smell can be. On the other hand, we can more or less agree that there are a few globally recognized "good" and "bad" smells. Name one person who dislikes the delicate perfume of a rose in bloom on a sunny day, for example.

But while we may agree on the power of scent to lift our spirits, how many of us actively consider it when we create our home environment? For such a powerful sense, smell is often largely overlooked as part of an interior scheme. You might light the odd scented candle or buy a bunch of flowers now and again, but would you like to know how to use scent to shape and improve your mood at home? If the answer is yes, read on.

Can Scent Improve Our Well-Being?

I set out to discover if there were universally accepted scents that could lower stress, increase happiness, and promote relaxation at home, and I started my research by talking to Roja Dove, master perfumer and a board director of the Fragrance Foundation, a group that promotes awareness and appreciation of scent. "Fragrance is one of the best things you can buy to make you feel good," he told me, "as each ingredient works on our subconscious, releasing hormones which, among other things, give us energy, lift our mood, or enhance sensations of pleasure."

Roja agrees that the link to memory is integral to the power that scent has on our mood. "A perfume brings back moments in our lives in vivid, glorious Technicolor," he says. "It has the ability to bring a smile to our lips or tears to our eyes; it can both repel us and attract us." So can we add to our memories and create new scent associations through the way we fragrance our homes? Roja thinks we can. "Our responses to scent are learned," he says, "each one locked away with a memory of association about whatever was happening to us at the time."

So could scent carry the key to happiness at home? Nicola Elliott, founder and creative director of wellness brand Neom Organics, thinks so. "Essential oils can be a natural antidote to the frenetic pace of life," she says, "and fragrance is so important for creating an atmosphere and emotion in the home."

"Fragrance is one of the best things you can buy to make you feel good."

The "happiest" scents

I asked Nicola and Roja to share their secrets for using the olfactory system for improving sleep quality, enhancing mood, and increasing energy at home with the pursuit of happiness in mind.

How to improve sleep

"There are countless studies that prove the relaxing qualities of lavender," says Nicola, and it is commonly used to encourage a good night's sleep, in both dried form and as an essential oil. Lavender is very easy to grow yourself, so if you have a balcony or terrace, try growing a small plant in a container (see page 74). "Jasmine is another deeply relaxing oil, known for its soothing properties," says Nicola. Roja also names chamomile, bergamot, rose, and sandalwood as essential oils that all have soothing, calming qualities "to help encourage sleep and relaxation."

How to extend energy

"Grapefruit, lemon, and rosemary are all excellent scents to help refresh and energize," says Nicola. "Citrus notes have been used for centuries to revive, uplift, inject life, and boost vitality," agrees Roja. "Think about the effect of someone peeling an orange in a stuffy train carriage—it instantly recharges the stale, stagnant air. Citrus notes are mainly used in the top notes of a fragrance, which means—like that orange—the burst of energy is short-lived. You have to spritz little and often to keep your boost going." It is actually possible to grow citrus fruit in cooler climates, if you keep them sheltered and protected during winter. The small lemon tree I have at home always heightens my mood, thanks to both the vibrant color of its fruit (see page 31) and the incredible scent of its blossoms in spring.

How to increase happiness

"Whatever your version of happiness is, we believe it starts with a positive state of mind," says Nicola. "Happiness means different things to different people, but you can definitely use essential oils to lift your spirits and inspire a little optimism." She suggests mimosa, white neroli, and lemon to improve your frame of mind, as well as energizing wild mint and uplifting mandarin to "help calm the body while improving circulation and boosting immunity." Roja adds, "Sandalwood has been proven in scientific trials to increase positive feelings, and vanilla is a psychogenic aphrodisiac that enhances positive sensations."

How to Choose the Right Scent for Each Room

Still not sure which scent you need? I asked Roja if there were certain scents that suited different rooms in the home. "Because of our individual interior styles, there are no hard-and-fast rules as to what scents work in what spaces," he admits, "though as a generalization, cosseting scents like amber and vanilla work wonderfully to create a cozy atmosphere for an evening in the living room, while gourmand scents, such as herbs, spices, and fruits, help keep a kitchen smelling fresh and full of flavor. Anything fresh works well in the bathroom, but overall you can never go wrong with the uplifting aroma of citrus notes in any room."

Create happy memories

"When we discover a scent we truly love, it will have ingredients within it that have positive, feel-good associations," says Roja. "The scent itself then becomes an odor that also has positive associations and makes us feel safe, secure, happy, and well."

Trust your instincts

"Most of all, listen to yourself," says Nicola, and trust your own instincts. "Choose scents that make you feel calm and content; your body knows best what your mind needs most."

"Your body knows best what your mind needs most."

A rose by any other name . . .

Could a floral scent be a quick shortcut to happiness? Quite possibly, according to research led by Jeannette Haviland-Jones, of Rutgers University, in New Jersey. As reported on LiveScience.com, the researchers ran an experiment in which they treated a room with a floral smell, a classic fragrance like Chanel No. 5 or Johnson's Baby Powder, or nonscented air. They then asked fifty-nine college students to write about three life events. The essays were then coded for the number of positive and negative words used. Participants in the floral-scented room used about three times as many happiness-related words in their writings. Time to splurge on a bunch of fresh flowers, perhaps?

Banish the Bad

Before you start adding beautiful scents to your home, you will need to banish any bad odors that might be lingering. Here's how to scrub your home clean.

Scour your refrigerator

Out-of-date food and spilled liquids can quickly create an offensive odor in a refrigerator, and you can't just cover it up. Keeping the contents of your refrigerator neatly labelled and organized is a good way to keep track of what you have and to avoid the unpleasant surprise of discovering a rotten tomato liquefying, forgotten on a shelf. It is also a good idea to give your refrigerator a good scrub every couple of months, removing all the shelves and giving them a hot soak in the sink while you wipe down the walls and the insides of the doors.

Put any cleaning cloths through a hot wash

Dishcloths, scrubbing brushes, and floor mops can soak up all kinds of nasty aromas, so get ahead of any bacteria buildup by putting them through a regular hot-wash cycle and replacing them frequently to keep them in tiptop condition.

Clean pet bedding

If you are a pet owner, you know how quickly animal smells can permeate soft furnishings, so staying on top of cleaning out litter trays and freshening up pet beds will probably be second nature to you. Storing a small hand-held vacuum cleaner close by to get rid of dog or cat hairs is a good idea, as is regularly washing your pet's bedding and any cloth toys on your washer's hot cycle.

Refresh flower water

If you have ever been away for a few days and left a vase of flowers in a window, you know how off-putting the odor can be on your return. Flower stems can decay quickly if left in direct sunlight, and the water can turn stale and slimy. Regularly refresh the water in your vases and try adding a (tiny) drop of bleach to kill off any bacteria (see page 79). And if you are going away for a few days, remember to empty your cut flowers into the compost bin before you leave.

Clean your washing machine

If you don't regularly clean your washing machine, you might notice that your clothes are not coming out as fresh as they should be. It is simple to fix, though; just remove the detergent tray once a week and scrub it to prevent any soap buildup, and add a cleaning agent to an empty hot wash once a month to get rid of any bacteria and leave it sparkling. You will also need to wipe down the rubber seal around the door after every couple of washes because stale water can accumulate there.

Unblock sinks and drains

Cleaning out sink and bathtub drains might not be the most glamorous job in the world, but you will need to tackle it in order to keep your home smelling fresh. Regularly clear out any drain traps, and once a month flush them with a cleaning agent and hot water to prevent blockages.

Eight Ways to Fragrance Your Home

Now that you have chosen the fragrances you want to bring into your home, here are a few ways to do so.

 Oil burner
An oil burner consists of a ceramic dish, into which you place a little water with a few drops of essential oil, over a tealight. When the tealight is lit, it warms the oil and releases the aroma into the room. Good for creating a soft, diffused scent, an oil burner also adds the reassuringly cozy twinkle of a little flame as it burns, making it a lovely addition to a mantelpiece on winter evenings. It does need watching, though, as the combination of flame and hot oil is a little risky anywhere that it might be knocked over or reached by children or pets. You also need to take care not to let it burn dry.

Naturally scented candle
A candle combines the cheerful flicker of a flame with the slow release of a fragrance and has the added benefit of looking beautiful when unlit, too. The choice out there is vast, ranging from small votives to large glass jars. But again, these obviously need to be kept away from children when lit and so are best suited to rooms that don't get lots of through traffic.

 Reed diffuser

Another way of releasing scent into a room without having to worry about candles or hot oil is to use a reed diffuser. This works by drawing up a scented solution from a glass jar via a bundle of thin reeds, which then releases a continuous stream of fragrance molecules into the air. To prevent any spillages, keep reed diffusers on a high shelf or tucked away out of the reach of small hands. They will quietly and effectively perfume the air all day long.

 Fresh flowers

The original is always the best. So when you can, invest in the living, breathing version of your favorite floral scent, be it a vase of bluebells, an armful of roses, or a sprig of jasmine. The scent will be much subtler than an artificial replica, but it will be all the fresher and more delightful for it. Plus, if you pick flowers from your own garden, they will also bring something of the scent of the damp earth, fresh breeze, or summer rain with them, which is something that really can't be bottled.

5 Windowsill herbs in the kitchen

Mint, lemon balm, basil . . . if you love the zingy, uplifting scents of these common garden herbs, try growing containers of them in your kitchen or dining room so you can cut them straight from the plant to make teas or flavor your cooking. I have an herb planter positioned near the door in my kitchen, as I like to gently brush my hand over the leaves on my way out in the morning to release the fresh, invigorating scent.

6 Dried lavender

Brushing past a pot of fresh lavender is a wonderful way to get a delicate hit of that heady fragrance, but this is one flower that works almost as well in dried form. You can either buy a bag of dried lavender or make your own by hanging up a bunch of freshly cut stems indoors, somewhere warm, and letting them gently dry out. Once dried, lavender can be bagged up in little sachets and used to scent drawers and closets—or try tucking one in with your freshly laundered bed linen.

Linen spray

For heavenly scented bedding, towels, and throws, a naturally fragranced linen spray is a lovely way to bring your favorite scent into your living room or bedroom. Spritz textiles between washes to keep them fresh, or on laundry just before ironing. Soothing aromas such as lavender can work wonderfully as a pillow mist before bed, too, if used sparingly.

"A freshly cooked loaf of bread or tray of cakes will create a cozy aroma, but if you lack the time or inclination to get baking, a vanilla candle or essential oil can have a similarly warming effect."

Ready, steady, bake . . .

Who doesn't like the smell of warm baked goods directly from the oven? Widely recommended by real estate agents as a surefire way to make your home seem more appealing to potential buyers, the scent of home baking has something deeply comforting about it. A just-baked loaf of bread or a tray of cupcakes will create a cozy aroma, but if you lack the time or inclination to get baking, a vanilla candle or essential oil can have a similarly warming effect.

Grow Your Own

While essential oils are a quick way to get a concentrated burst of fragrance at home, there are many scented plants that you can grow in your own garden if you like the idea of a truly natural fragrance and have time to experiment. The following plants are all richly scented, and some can even be grown in containers.

Garden plants

Mock orange (*Philadelphus*)

Jasmine (*Jasminum*)

Honeysuckle (*Lonicera*)

Roses (*Rosa*)

Eucalyptus (*Eucalyptus*)

Container plants

Lavender (*Lavandula*)

Rosemary (*Rosmarinus officinalis*)

Mint (*Mentha*)

Sweet peas (*Lathyrus odoratus*)

Hyacinth (*Hyacinthus*)

Right plant, right place

Repeat the above mantra when choosing which flowers to grow in a bed or border. The key is to identify your soil type, note how much sun the area gets, and then choose plants that will be happiest in those conditions. Ask at a local plant nursery for advice, or use an online tool such as the RHS Plant Finder or Dave's Garden. Alternatively, take a stroll around your neighborhood and discover which plants are growing well for your neighbors—chances are these will do well in your garden, too!

Cultivate containers

With container plants you can be a little more adventurous, as you can control the environment. So, if you hanker after lavender but don't have the right soil conditions, plant a large terracotta pot with a good potting mix and plenty of drainage. The flip side is that a container will need more love and attention than a garden bed, as you cannot let the soil dry out or become too waterlogged.

6

Harness the Mood-Boosting Power of Flowers

There are few things that can lift my spirits as quickly and effectively as a bunch of freshly picked garden flowers. From the rich scent of roses and delicate sweet peas to gently swaying stems of foxgloves and stately delphiniums, my home looks happier and my mood feels brighter when I take the time to fill a vase with flowers.

If you feel the same way, there is a very good reason for that: These colorful little mood enhancers have actually been scientifically proven to increase our happiness at home. According to one study at Rutgers University, published in the journal *Evolutionary Psychology*, the presence of flowers has an immediate and long-term effect on emotional reactions, mood, social behaviors, and even memory.

If you want to get a little of that flower power in your own home, here's how to harness some of their mood-boosting magic.

Petal Power

How to Keep Your Flowers Alive Longer

Part of the appeal of a bouquet of flowers is, for me, that the blooms have such a transient beauty. Watching a tightly closed flower bud unfurl into a deliciously scented rose over the course of a few short days, seeing it bloom into beauty and then gently fade, compels me to appreciate it fully during the brief period it is at its peak.

There are, however, a few ways to encourage your cut flowers to last a bit longer indoors. I asked Stuart Fenwick, resident floral artist at the UK-based flower delivery company, bloomon, to share his top tips for keeping your flowers alive as long as possible.

Don't hang about

Speed is your friend when it comes to arranging cut flowers. For store-bought blooms, you'll want to get them into water as soon as possible, so as soon as you get them home, immediately remove them from the packaging, cut the stems, and plunge them into a bucket of cool water.

Cut stems at an angle

Cut 1 inch (2.5 cm) off your flower stems at an angle with a clean, sharp knife, pair of scissors, or pruning shears; do this every time you change the water (see opposite), because the ends of the stems will quickly seal up, preventing fresh water from being drawn up into the flower. Flowers or foliage with woody stems will need extra help to draw water, so use a knife to slice the stem vertically up the center, which will maximize the surface area of the stem that has contact with the water.

Stay cool

Windowsills are common surfaces for displaying flowers, but it is actually much better for your blooms to be kept out of direct sunlight and away from radiators or any other heat sources. Flowers kept cool will open at a slower rate and will last longer.

Add some bleach

A drop of bleach in the flower water will help keep your flowers fresh by killing any bacteria. Change the water every three days, adding no more than a drop of bleach each time to prolong the life of your flowers.

Keep water levels low

It can be tempting to fill a vase to the brim with water, but this is actually detrimental to the life of your flowers, as it speeds up the rate at which the stems will start to deteriorate. Instead, just add a small amount of water to your vase. The only exception to this rule is if your bouquet contains woody stems; these need all the water they can get and so will appreciate a deep drink.

Strip excess leaves

Strip away any excess foliage
from below the rim of the vase,
and make sure no leaves or foliage
are submerged, as this will lead to
murky water and slimy flower stems.

Don't mix flowers with fruit

Flowers and fruit can look beautiful together,
but they are not really the best of friends.
Many fruits, including apples and pears, give
off ethylene gas, which will make the flowers
deteriorate faster, so keep your blooms well
away from the fruit bowl if you want them to
last longer indoors.

How to Arrange the Perfect Bouquet

Here are a few quick tips that will help you create the perfect bouquet at home.

- Place your vase in front of you and use it to roughly measure the height of each flower stem before you cut it.
- Strip away all the foliage that will sit below the neck of the vase to prevent premature rot.
- Place your flowers in the vase one by one, at an angle, creating a tripod shape; turn your vase as you work so you can view the bouquet from different angles.

- Vary the height of the flower stems to create movement and life (unless, of course, you are aiming for a tightly ordered arrangement of one type of flower displayed en masse).
- Place the tallest and sturdiest stems in the very center of the vase to avoid the gap that can appear when less robust flower stems fall to the edges of the vase.

Blooming Lovely

Here's how to choose and arrange flowers to suit your interior style.

If your home is contemporary

> *"If you want to make an impact, go large with your display and let it take center stage."*

Stick to one shade

If your interior style is clean-lined and contemporary, stick to one color of flower and go large with it to create a really striking display. Tall spikes of crimson red crocosmia would look wonderful in a simple glass vase, for example, as would a beautiful cluster of sky-blue delphiniums. The secret is to pick flowers with strong, clean lines and a saturated color and give them the space to shine, without competition from other shapes and hues.

Choose structural foliage

It always pays to consider foliage if you want to create a sculptural display, so think about grasses and leaves as well as flower heads. Mix them in with flower stems or display them as sculptural forms in their own right. A bunch of eucalyptus stems always makes for an elegant display and will give your room a beautifully fresh aroma, too.

Play with scale

A cluster of small flower arrangements can look whimsical and fun, but if you want to make an impact, go large with your display and let it take center stage. An oversized vase filled with sculptural grasses, lush foliage, and bold flower heads will shine in a minimal interior, and will usually be all the ornament you need to create impact in an entrance hallway or on a dining table.

Find streamlined vases

Patterned vases or repurposed vessels, such as teacups, are perfect for a relaxed, country-style interior (see pages 84 and 85), but if you want to create a sleek display, steer clear of patterned or vintage-shaped vases and choose a large, streamlined vase instead, in either clear glass or a single block color, for the greatest impact.

If your home is country

Fill a ceramic jug

A glazed ceramic water jug in a bright, cheerful color is the perfect vessel for a country-style floral display. I have far too many of these in my own home, as I can't stop collecting them every time I see one. Handmade jugs are perfect, as they have that all-important wobbly appearance, and a hand-applied glaze or hand-painted finish also adds a dash of character.

Choose a mix of multicolored wildflowers

Country-style is my personal favorite way of displaying flowers in my own home. I like to create a cheerful mix of different shapes, colors, and sizes, drawing heavily on homegrown flowers or foraging finds, which tend to be more delicate and whimsical than nursery flowers or store-bought ones. A country-style flower display is the polar opposite of the neatly formal displays you tend to see in more traditional interiors (see pages 86–87), so use a variety of stem heights to create movement and life. Cottage-garden flowers such as foxgloves (*Digitalis*), lupines (*Lupinus*), and old-fashioned roses (*Rosa*) are essential to this look.

Celebrate foraged treasures

If you are able to forage locally without damaging wildlife habitats, there are treasures to be found in the wild. I like to collect armfuls of frothy cow parsley (*Anthriscus sylvestris*) in the spring and branches of red and gold leaves and deep scarlet berries in the autumn. Displaying local, seasonal finds will help anchor you to the landscape and stay in tune with nature.

Mix and match vases and containers

Country-style flower arranging is relaxed and free, so it lends itself beautifully to a mix-and-match approach to vases and containers. A lively assortment of teacups, cans, and bottles filled with local flora will create a fun and happy display, so use whatever you have on hand and celebrate anything quirky, colorful, or vintage in pattern and style.

> *"Displaying local, seasonal finds will help anchor you to the landscape and stay in tune with nature."*

If your home is traditional

Fill a shallow bowl with roses
A cut-glass bowl filled with beautiful roses makes a chic, timeless floral display and is a quick way to enhance your interior. Perfect for placing on a formal hallway table alongside a cluster of shiny silver photo frames, or for adding a dash of understated glamor to a polished wood coffee table, this classic look whispers refinement rather than shouts it.

Create large centerpiece displays
In a restful, neatly organized, traditional interior, small groups of containers can look messy and cluttered, so if you crave order and calm, create one large display rather than lots of little ones, and stick to a couple of types of flowers to prevent the display from having a wild look that would be more at home in a country-style interior. Cream-colored roses, green and white hydrangea heads, and straight-stemmed dahlias are all classic flower choices for a restrained display.

Celebrate orchids
One flower that doesn't need any clever arranging or further adornment is the orchid. These flowers ooze elegance and glamor and will add a layer of sophistication to any room they grace with their presence. Their sculptural form and glacial beauty are perfectly matched to a traditional interior. Try displaying a single orchid on a bedside table, or a cluster of three or five on a polished wood table as a showstopping centerpiece.

> *"If you crave order and calm, create one large display rather than lots of little ones, and stick to a couple of types of flowers to prevent the display from having a wild look."*

Six Vase Ideas That Won't Cost You a Penny

 Empty liquor bottles
I was on a flight with a friend recently when she ordered a gin and tonic. The miniature measure of gin arrived in the prettiest sky-blue bottle and as soon as it was empty I popped it in my carry-on luggage, because I knew it would make the cutest flower vase. And so it does. I use it in the winter to display the first of the tiny delicate snowdrops (*Galanthus*) and hellebores (*Helleborus*), and in the summer I fill it with delicate sweet peas (*Lathyrus odoratus*) or a couple of stems of lavender (*Lavandula*). Larger liquor bottles make excellent vases, too; gin, in particular, tends to come in wonderful green or blue glass bottles. Ask friends and family to save them for you, or treat it as an excuse to throw a cocktail party and keep the empties.

 Decorative tin cans

Some tins and cans are just too pretty to throw away, so make a point of saving any antique containers or unusual food cans to reuse as flower vases. Old-fashioned olive oil cans or vintage mustard cans are unlikely but effective vases. Even humble tomato or baked bean cans can be repurposed, too—just wash off the label if it isn't particularly appealing and give the metal beneath a coat of paint, or tie on a length of pretty fabric or ribbon to liven it up.

 Jam jars

Glass jars make ideal vases for small, country-style arrangements, and you can usually find one or two in every food pantry. Give them a good scrub when they are empty, then fill them with a mix of pretty wildflowers, cut short so the flower heads sit just above the rim. Twist some wire around the lip of the jar and curve it up and over to create a little handle, and you have created the perfect hanging vase for decorating an outdoor party.

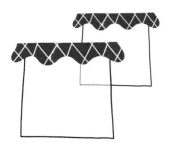

Glass makeup bottles

Empty foundation bottles or glass perfume bottles make lovely little vases for mini bouquets. Perfume bottles, in particular, tend to be interesting shapes and beautiful colors, so a little cluster of them filled with a mix of small wildflowers would make a lovely vintage-style display.

5 An ice bucket

If you need a large vase but don't have one on hand, an ice bucket can make an excellent stand-in. They usually have straight sides or flare out slightly at the top, so are ideal for holding a large bunch of tall flowers and creating a dramatic centerpiece.

6 Teacups

Delicate vintage teacups are perfect for displaying old-fashioned roses; a cluster of mismatched floral-patterned teacups filled with large scented roses would make a whimsical display for a summer tea party. You will need to cut the stems very short, and you may also need to fix them in place with a grid of tape (see below for details), but they will lend a pretty elegance to your table.

TOP TIP

If you have a wide-necked vase or bowl and you're struggling to keep your flower arrangement looking neat, here's a secret florist tip to keep your blooms in place. Make a grid across the top of the container by laying strips of slim masking tape horizontally and then vertically from one side of the rim to the other. The neat grid of little squares will serve as a framework to hold your flowers. Build your display by placing individual stems into the gaps between the tape to structure; the grid will keep each bloom firmly but gently in place.

How to Grow Your Own

If you want to have a cheap and local supply of flowers all year round, why not grow a few yourself? You don't need a huge garden for this; in fact, you don't even need a garden, because many flowers can be grown in patio containers or balcony plant pots.

I asked Professor Alistair Griffiths, director of Science and Collections at the Royal Horticultural Society (RHS), which plants he considers the easiest to grow for total beginners, and he recommended a simple mix of four different bulbs (see below). The fact that they are perennial bulbs means they will come up year after year in a container, so once you have planted them you can just let them do their thing.

Perennial bulbs for a year-round flower supply

Spring: Daffodils (*Narcissus*)
There are few sights more cheering than the first daffodils of spring, heralding the return of warmer days.

Summer: Purple Alliums (*Allium*)
These large purple flowers make a striking display in a summer garden and are wonderful as a cut flower to take indoors, too.

Autumn: Crocuses (*Crocus*)
For a lively splash of color just as the rest of the garden is fading, plant a cluster of autumn-flowering crocus bulbs during the summer months.

Winter: Snowdrops (*Galanthus*)
Planting just a few snowdrop bulbs in late spring will reward you with little points of brilliant white light the following winter.

Shine a Light on Well-Being

There is one very unlikely room in my home that I have ended up using almost more than any other, and the reason why has everything to do with the subject of this chapter.

The space in question is a tiny little guest room at the back of the house, but from midday onward on a clear day it is bathed in the warmest golden sunshine. When the doors are open, the birds are singing, and the trees are gently swaying outside, it becomes a glorious, peaceful, sun-drenched space—and my absolute favorite place to be. This chapter provides some inspiration on ways that you, too, can bring the sunshine indoors.

Can Natural Light Make Us Happier and Healthier?

The mood-boosting qualities of my little guest room made me wonder if the amount of natural daylight we get in our homes has a direct correlation to our mood, happiness, and general well-being. I decided to see if I could uncover any proven links between the amount of daylight in the home and health and happiness levels. To help me do so, I spoke to Dr. Phyllis Zee, director of Sleep Medicine at Northwestern Medicine in Chicago who has undertaken research into this very topic in collaboration with the University of Illinois.

Dr. Zee found that office workers who have more exposure to natural light in the workplace had longer sleep duration, better sleep quality, more physical activity, and a better quality of life compared to office workers with less exposure to natural light in the workplace. But do these findings carry over into our homes? "We studied the office environment because we spend so much of the daytime indoors at work," Dr. Zee explained to me, "but yes, the same theory applies to homes." Why exactly does daylight have such a big impact on our health? "Light is the most important time giver for internal timing," says Dr. Zee, "and thus can positively or negatively affect health—depending on the time of exposure."

Good day sunshine!

According to Dr. Zee's research, timing is everything when it comes to light levels in the home, and morning light can have a huge impact on our health and happiness. "Morning light has been shown to be particularly important for mood, sleep, and weight regulation," she says. "If possible, you should try to sit or work next to a window in the morning," advises Dr. Zee, "and have breakfast near a window."

If this really isn't possible, the next best alternative is to choose bright artificial lighting (white broad-spectrum) for your most-trafficked areas. Light should be about 1000 lux, according to Dr. Zee, and you can measure the level with a light meter, or even with some smartphones.

Wind down naturally

"While light exposure in the morning and during the day is beneficial," says Dr. Zee, "exposure during the evening is actually detrimental to sleep, and perhaps metabolism." To help your body wind down naturally and prepare for sleep, Dr. Zee suggests you start to dim your lights at home from about 8 p.m. (On light summer evenings, start to draw the curtains.) "This is the time that, for most people, their own melatonin, produced by the pineal gland, begins to rise, to help signal darkness to the body," she explains. "Bright light exposure late in the evening will block secretion of this natural hormone of darkness."

(To find out more about how to create the perfect environment for sleep, take a look at pages 49–61.)

"Timing is everything when it comes to light levels in the home, and morning light can have a huge impact on our health and happiness."

Let There Be Light

Nine Ways to Flood Your Home with Mood-Boosting Sunlight

Most people feel better with the warmth of the sun on their faces; here's how to maximize the amount of natural daylight in your home.

 Reflect light with mirrors
Mirrors can work magic in a dark interior, so hang them liberally on your walls and watch your daylight double. Place them opposite sunny windows to reflect light, or on walls directly underneath skylights to magnify the effect. Mirrors also work particularly well in dark, narrow hallways, and it can pay to choose the largest one you can afford for this typically shadowy and sunless space. If your budget is tight, you could have a piece of mirror cut to size by a glass specialist. If you need to cover a large area, doing it this way will often work out to be more cost-effective than buying a regular mirror, and you can usually choose from a range of finishes, from crystal clear to delicately "foxed" (the name for that beautifully marbled finish you see on antique mirrors). You can also help scatter sunlight by choosing a faceted mirror, or add an unexpected twist with a wall of reflective mirrored tiles in a kitchen or bathroom.

> *"Mirrors can work magic in a dark interior, so hang them liberally on your walls and watch your daylight double."*

2 Choose a front door with a glass panel

A heavy front door will obviously block all light from entering your home, but replacing it with a glass-paneled door can transform a dark entryway and draw extra daylight into a gloomy interior. If you are worried about privacy, choose frosted or etched glass for the panels and pull a curtain across at night. Stained-glass panels are a beautiful option for a front door, as they have the power to transform daylight as it travels through from outside to inside. I saw a beautiful stained-glass panel designed in a sunburst pattern in a house I visited several years ago. As light filtered through the yellow and orange glass panels from outside, it was changed into beams of rich golden sunlight that brightened the narrow hallway beyond.

3 Clear cluttered windowsills

Sweep clutter off your windowsills and scrub them clean to allow as much light to reach inside as possible. It may sound like a small change, but you would be surprised how much a windowsill display of photo frames, vases, or ornaments can eat into the window space and reduce the amount of light streaming through. Place your ornaments elsewhere and polish the windowsills to a shine to ensure maximum light reflection. Another obvious but easy fix for increasing sunlight in an interior is to ensure your windows are sparkling clean. Give them a regular scrub to counteract the buildup of dirt and grime, and the quality of light should improve.

4 Replace solid interior doors with glass-paneled ones

An open-plan layout is the obvious way to maximize natural daylight indoors, but if that is not an option, there are several ways to achieve the same effect without getting demolition-happy. Swapping solid interior doors for glass ones is an easy way to allow light to penetrate from one room to the next while still providing a clear division. Internal windows are another option and are worth asking your architect or builder to consider if you are about to start any renovation work. The aim of these interior windows is to link areas of the house and allow light to make its way from one room to another. Most homes have internal walls, doors, or hallways blocking the center of the space, but if you can connect rooms—front to back or side to side—with glass doors or windows, it will let light travel from one to the other as the sun moves overhead throughout the day, allowing the darker rooms to "borrow" daylight from the sunnier ones in the morning, and vice versa in the evening.

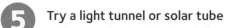

5 Try a light tunnel or solar tube

To increase luminosity in a dark room with little or no natural light, a solar tube or light tunnel can be a very effective option and a good alternative to installing artificial light. Ideal for a basement, a hallway, or an internal room with no outward-facing windows, they can funnel light down from outside and wash a dark room with daylight. Again, these are probably only an option to consider if you are about to start renovation work, but they really can transform a windowless space, so ask your architect or builder about the possibility of adding one.

6 Open up the stairs

Top floors will be brighter than lower floors in many houses, so think about how you can pull some of this natural light down via your staircase. Choosing open-riser stairs will allow slivers of light to make their way down from upper floors. Alternatively, painting your stair treads in a light-toned paint is another way to help bounce light down each step to lower floors. Mirrors, again, are useful here, and a mirrored staircase wall will work wonders in reflecting light from upper floors and directing it down into the rest of the house. If you are about to undertake a redesign, adding a light well to a staircase can be an effective way of brightening up a gloomy stairwell and shining light down into lower floors, so ask your architect or builder if this could be an option.

7 **Hang curtains so they pull completely away from the window when open**

A secret designer tip when hanging drapes is to choose a curtain rod that extends out beyond the sides of the window frame, so when you draw the curtains back you pull them clear of the window and they rest against the wall instead of the edges of the window frame. This allows you to keep the entire width of the window clear and will ensure maximum daylight gets in. The same goes for blinds: Choose the kind that pull up and away from the window, rather than ones that sit within the window frame.

8 **Choose reflective materials**

In addition to mirrors, many other materials have light-reflecting qualities, so consider bringing some into your room scheme to help scatter more light around. This doesn't have to mean lots of hard-edged materials like glass and metal, though; glossy paint finishes, metallic frames, highly polished wood surfaces, and light-colored flooring will all help maximize every scrap of daylight that makes its way into the room. Dark colors and matte textures will have the opposite effect, so save those for spaces where you want to evoke a cocooning feeling.

9 **Look to the sky**

If you are overshadowed by other buildings or if your windows are not quite pulling in the amount of light you would like, a skylight could be your new best friend. Rather than relying on the few hours of sunlight that come through the window each day, an overhead skylight will offer more hours of consistent daylight. By pulling light directly down from above, the light quality is often much better than that supplied by a vertical window, too. They are also great options for a single-story building or a loft conversion.

Liven It Up
Three Ways to Brighten a Gloomy View

Sometimes it just is not possible to throw your windows open or leave them uncovered for large parts of the day. Unappealing views or privacy concerns in urban areas can mean you need to keep your curtains closed or blinds down all day long, and some people may have pets or children to keep safe. If either is the case in your home, don't worry: Pick one of these window treatments that still allow the daylight in.

1 **Clever window film**
Window film is a great, low-cost choice for screening a window while still letting natural light through. There are lots of fun options available, from bespoke designs to patterns you can order by the yard, and they are a good way to add personality to a room. When I redecorated my bathroom I wanted to replace the roller blinds, which were cutting into the window space, so I installed a window film with a subtle metallic finish instead. The film has tiny silver particles embedded in it, which lend a dazzling luminosity to the light as it filters through. I chose a design flecked with tiny cutout stars, which allow small slivers of light to glint through and scatter pinpoints of sunshine around the room in the morning. For such a little amount of money, this window treatment has absolutely transformed the small space, so it's a great option if you are short on time or funds. It's also an ideal solution for a rented home, as it's easy to install and remove.

Smart shutters

2 Shutters with adjustable slats are useful for controlling the light or privacy levels in a room throughout the day because they can be opened or closed as required and angled to let the light in while still providing privacy from outside. They also look timeless, and you can choose from a range of colors and finishes, including natural wood, classic white, bright primaries, and soft pastels. Lighter colors will give you maximum reflective powers, and a glossy finish can add extra luminosity.

Sheer fabric

3 If you prefer the flutter of a curtain at your window, a sheer, light-colored linen is a good option for screening a window without completely blocking the light. A lightweight, open-weave fabric will draw a soft veil over an unattractive view or screen your interior from people looking in, while still allowing diffused light to filter through. A soft fabric will also pleasingly catch the breeze if the window is open—a good way to bring life and movement to a gloomy space.

"A soft fabric will also pleasingly catch the breeze if the window is open."

Follow the Sun

How to Design Your Rooms Around the Direction of Sunlight

Often we accept our floor plans and room layouts as fixed entities when we move into a new home, without stopping to think if they are the best solutions for us. But with this new knowledge about the power of natural illumination, it could be time to overhaul your floor plan and shake up your room layouts.

Consider for a moment the way the sun travels, rising in the east and setting in the west. In terms of your home, that means an east-facing room will get sunlight first thing in the morning, while a west-facing room will remain in shade, and vice versa in the evening. So far, so logical. But do you use the rooms in a way that makes the most of this pattern, or are you fighting against it without realizing?

For example, in an ideal world you would start your day in an east-facing room to take advantage of the morning sunlight, and then move to a west-facing room later in the day to bask in the mellow, late-afternoon sunshine. While it might not be possible to drastically alter the layout of your home, take a look at your floor plans and consider if there are any small tweaks you could make to enable you to follow the sun around your home. Is it possible to eat breakfast in an east-facing room, for example? Could you move your evening sitting room to a west-facing space?

"An east-facing room will get sunlight first thing in the morning, while a west-facing room will remain in shade, and vice versa in the evening."

North, east, south, or west . . . which is best?

Here's how to chase the sun

In the northern hemisphere, north-facing rooms tend to get a cooler, blue-toned natural light, so try to designate them for areas that get the least use, such as laundry rooms, bathrooms, or storage spaces. (This applies to south-facing rooms in the southern hemisphere.)

East-facing rooms tend to have warmer light in the mornings and colder light in the evenings, and so are ideal for breakfast rooms or bedrooms, if you like to wake up with the sun.

South-facing rooms (in the northern hemisphere) usually get the highest levels of warm natural light, so it makes sense to use them for living spaces and family rooms.

West-facing rooms tend to feel colder in the mornings and warmer in the evenings as the sun travels, so they are perfect for evening living spaces.

8

How to Create a Cozy Retreat

One of the most cherished memories I can recall is of curling up in front of a large open fire, watching the flames dance and flicker, feeling the warmth on my face, and listening to the soft rise and fall of family chatter all around. This feeling of contentment had as much to do with being surrounded by the security and comfort of family as it did with the crackle of the logs in the grate, the warmth of the flames, and the softness of the rug beneath me.

So, it is my view that a cozy room has to have three essential elements: warmth, texture, and security. Security, for me, is the feeling of being safe and surrounded by close friends and family, while warmth and texture can be anything from ambient lighting and soft materials to the snug retreat of a reading nook. In this chapter I have looked at ways of increasing the cozy factor at home and creating a space that nourishes and nurtures.

Staying In Is the New Going Out

Five Quick Ways to Create a Cozy Home on a Budget

> "Use a variety of tactile elements to create a soft, enveloping space in which to hibernate as the nights draw in."

1 Choose natural textures

The secret to a cozy room scheme is to use a variety of tactile elements to create a soft, enveloping space in which to hibernate as the nights draw in. Steer clear of anything hard-edged or cold—such as metal, glass, or concrete—and choose soft, natural materials instead to create a room that invites you to settle in and relax. Everything you use on a daily basis should be made of simple but good-quality materials, so when you are choosing a new throw, pillow, or even a mug, think about how the material feels as well as how it looks. Polished wood, hand-glazed pottery, soft cottons, and crisp linens are all worth investing in, and any materials that you have frequent contact with, such as door handles or light pulls, for example, should be considered carefully, too.

2 Layer up

The key to staying warm on a chilly day is to dress yourself in several thin layers, so think of your home in the same way—and layer, layer, layer. In your living room, drape a soft throw over the arm of your sofa so you can easily reach for it if the temperature drops, and pile up a couple of large, soft pillows to snuggle into. Add in a thick pair of woollen socks and a mug of something warm and you are approaching perfection. In your bedroom, try layering fresh linen sheets with a plump cotton or velvet blanket, or keep a soft wool throw folded over the foot of the bed for extra warmth.

3 Create pools of light

A bright overhead strip light or LED spotlights will create clear, functional light for cooking or working at home, but when you want to switch to cozy mode, choose warm-toned yellow light and build up soft layers of it. The aim is to create a welcoming wash of light, so bring in a couple of table and floor lamps for an array of warm illumination sources. Choose warm-toned lightbulbs or select lampshades with a gold or yellow interior to create an enveloping circle of golden light (see also page 26).

4 String it out

Romantic string lights can create a warming effect if you choose ones with yellow-toned rather than brilliant-white bulbs. Curl them into a large glass jar to create a diffused glow or weave them around an unlit fireplace to give the illusion of warmth. You can also twist ropes of small lights along the top of a mantel or shelf and they will scatter tiny points of warm light around the room.

5 Treat your toes

If you have hardwood, tile, or laminate flooring, you will need to warm it up when the temperature drops, and so a thick-pile rug is your best friend here. Choose the softest ones you can find and place them anywhere your bare feet might hit the chilly ground, such as beside the bed or sofa. The secret to choosing the best rug is always to buy the largest one you can afford; a common mistake is to opt for a little square of a rug and place it directly in front of a chair. If a large rug is out of your budget (and they can be pricey), build up a patchwork of smaller, cheaper rugs to create the effect of one large rug. Run these rugs right underneath the sofa or bed to visually anchor the furniture, make the room look larger, and dramatically up the cozy factor.

Ten Lessons to Learn from the Danes

Denmark is widely held up as the happiest nation in the world, and much has been made of the Danes' concept of *hygge*—a word that describes the ideal cozy and snug atmosphere for the long winter months. It is interesting to consider, however, that hygge came out of a country that is also renowned for its love of minimalism and restrained, monochromatic interiors. So how do the two knit together, and how does their pairing affect happiness? I asked Danish design journalist Kasper Iversen to shed some light on the concept.

The secret to hygge

"It can seem as if there's a conflict between hygge and Scandi minimalism, as on the surface many elements seem completely opposite," says Kasper. "Hygge is about coziness, whereas minimalism is about clearing out everything that's not absolutely essential." But he believes there is a common thread between the two and it is *this* that's essential to the Danish way of life.

"Both hygge and minimalism embody a desire to keep things simple and uncomplicated," he says. "Minimalism is about not having more than you need, and hygge is about enjoying life through simple pleasures." So if you keep this ease of living in mind when creating your home, you are on the way to discovering what makes Danes so happy. "Don't make it complicated. Don't make it stressful," Kasper says. "That's the secret to the Danish way of life and the secret to hygge."

Here are Kasper's top ten tips for creating a hygge atmosphere at home.

Choose natural textiles

Textiles should be natural, hard-wearing, and unpretentious in order to create a sense of hygge. "The key thing to ask yourself is, 'Will it be ruined by a spilled drink?'" says Kasper. If you are worried about expensive fabrics being damaged, then you won't be able to truly relax, so choose washable cotton and linen slipcovers for sofas and armchairs, and steer clear of delicate silks and expensive velvets, as "these are really not hygge."

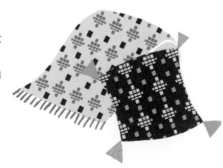

2 Cook simple meals

"Formal dining can never be hygge," says Kasper. The aim is to create a relaxed, intimate atmosphere, so the last thing you want to worry about is cooking an overblown dinner that makes you anxious. Prepare something easy that you have cooked many times before, and focus on spending time with your companions, rather than fussing over a hot stove in the kitchen.

3 Create cozy lighting

"You don't want your lighting to be too bright," says Kasper. To create a welcoming and enveloping feeling, layer warm, yellow-toned light sources, such as table or floor lamps, and avoid bright overhead lights.

4 Light a candle

Does the amount of hygge correlate to the number of candles you light? I put the question to Kasper, who advised moderation. "By all means, light one or two candles to create atmosphere, but don't go out and buy thirty candles because you think that is what's expected," he says. "Just use what you have on hand and what you think is cozy."

5 Bake it to make it

"Hygge is a feeling," says Kasper, so you need to consider all the senses when creating a cozy atmosphere, and scent is an important one. "Hygge is like a home-baked cake," he says—a warm, comforting scent that typifies a lazy afternoon spent indoors. If you want to get that soothing, home-sweet-home feeling for yourself, ramp up the nostalgic scents with a fresh loaf of bread or a vanilla cake.

"You need to consider all the senses when creating a cozy atmosphere."

6 Take your time

You can't hurry hygge. "It's all about being relaxed," says Kasper, "so you can't hygge if you're feeling stressed or in a rush." For instance, when entertaining, don't put too much pressure on yourself by trying to host too many people, or by organizing anything too elaborate. Keep things effortless and uncomplicated and allow yourself plenty of time to ease into a relaxed and mellow mindset.

7 Buy one good cake

"If you've invited friends over for coffee, there's no need to worry about buying lots of different treats for your guests," says Kasper. "Just buy one type of pastry that you really love and serve that—keep it simple and easy."

8 Put down roots

"Wood is very hygge," says Kasper, who describes the material as "down-to-Earth." It's much softer than hard-edged surfaces, such as glass or concrete, and will do much to create a relaxed, atmosphere at home. So bring in a wooden table, wooden dining chairs, or even wooden accessories, such as candlesticks or bowls, to create a warm and welcoming home environment.

9 Focus on friendship

Spending time with people you like and feel comfortable with is at the heart of hygge. "Hygge is something you can only do with people you feel relaxed around," agrees Kasper. So an evening spent with close friends or family is perfect. Inviting someone over with the express purpose of impressing them is the polar opposite of hygge, as is spending time with someone you feel anxious around, so focus on your close friends and family and those that you can totally unwind with.

10 Embrace imperfection

"Trying too hard to make something 'perfect' is stressful and not relaxing, so it goes against the concept of hygge," Kasper says. Don't try to create what you think others consider perfect; instead, give yourself permission to fashion an environment that you like and that makes you happy. "The 'perfect' home is the one where you feel comfortable," says Kasper. So whether you are having a light meal around your kitchen table or a cup of coffee and a catch-up with a friend, don't fuss about producing some immaculate event. If your dinner plates are mismatched or the meal doesn't turn out quite as you'd planned, let it go and appreciate a serene evening at home instead.

The Joy of Candles, Real Fires, and Wood-Burners

How to Fill Your Home with Warmth

A roaring fire on a dark winter's evening will hold a magnetic draw for everyone in a room; once you get a cheerful blaze going you'll find that competition is fierce for the closest seat to the hearth. Even a rug in front of the fireplace can be considered prime position for stretching out before the flames and daydreaming. Listening to the comforting crackle and whisper of the log fire is the ultimate in comfort.

Whether you are lucky enough to have an open fire in your home or not, there are several ways to bring the flickering warmth and caveman-coziness of fire into your living space. Here's how.

Focus on the fire

There is something beautifully mesmerizing about the flickering flames and happy crackle of a log fire, and if you have an open fireplace or wood-burning stove in your living space, you absolutely must give it the pride of place it deserves. Get it cleaned out and in top working condition and start thinking of it as the centerpiece of your room. Often the TV gets all the consideration in a living room and becomes the focal point for the arrangement of furniture. However, to design the coziest room possible, forget about the TV for a moment. Think instead of the fireplace as the center of attention, and ensure the flames can be seen (and the warmth felt) from every seat in the room. Make sure the fire is easy to light, which means keeping the hearth freshly swept, the logs ready-laid, and a stack of extra firewood close by, so as soon as there is the slightest chill in the air you can simply put a match to it and get a blaze going in no time.

"There is something beautifully mesmerizing about the flickering flames and happy crackle of a log fire."

Fill a fireplace

If you have a decorative fireplace, rather than a working one, you can still create the effect of a cheerful log fire by filling the fireplace with a cluster of church candles to mimic the dancing warmth of a real fire. Alternatively, fill an empty fireplace with a stack of freshly chopped logs and weave a string of lights in between them to create a twinkling focal point and bring a little of the warmth and fragrance of firewood into your living space.

Branch out

Firelight can bring warmth and life to other rooms in your home, too, so consider enjoying the cheerful glow of a candle in your kitchen, dining room, or bathroom. A simple candlestick on a kitchen table will add atmosphere and cozy warmth to mealtimes, while a couple of candles in glass jars in a bathroom will create

a comforting spa-like feel at bath times. If you are worried about the risk of fire, make a "safety candle" by placing a small votive candle in a glass jar filled with sand or water (it will float on top); the candle will extinguish itself when it has burned down. That said, never, ever leave a candle burning when there is no one in the room.

How to Create a Reading Nook

Give me a good book and a comfy chair and I am very happy. My idea of cozy perfection is a dedicated reading nook, piled up with deep, comfy cushions and surrounded by stacks of books. If you would like to squeeze a dedicated reading space into your home, here are four ways to create your own library nook.

1 **Take over a corner**
Is there a quiet corner in your home that you can reclaim as a reading spot? It's important to choose somewhere peaceful and, ideally, away from the main living room. It doesn't have to be a large space; the best reading nooks are snug. So as long as there is enough space to tuck in a chair and a lamp, it will work. Potentially overlooked corners to consider are stairway landings, guest bedrooms, or dining rooms. Get your thinking hat on and look at your home with fresh eyes to locate the perfect nook.

2 **Transform a closet**
This might sound a little unusual, but a closet can actually make an ideal reading nook. If you are able to clear out a hallway, bedroom, or playroom closet, you then just need to take down any internal shelves and remove the door and you have an instant cocoon-like den. Pile in plenty of comfy floor cushions and install some good, welcoming lighting and you have created the perfect reading nook for children. Or, if you have a little more time and budget and want to create a grown-up reading nook, ask a carpenter to build a raised seating bench into the closet space and line it with plump pillows to create a cushy retreat where you can hide away from the hustle and bustle of daily life.

③ Light it right

To create the perfect cozy corner you will want to avoid really bright overhead lighting, but you do need good enough light to read by. A wall-mounted reading lamp is perfect for a closet nook, and a floor lamp will do the trick in a nestled corner. For a children's reading nook, try stringing ropes of lights across the ceiling of the space to create a magical, den-like atmosphere, in addition to supplying a dedicated reading light.

> "My idea of cozy perfection is a dedicated reading nook, piled up with deep, comfy cushions and surrounded by stacks of books."

④ Be inspired by Harry Potter

The awkward triangle of storage space under the stairs is often used for little more than coat or shoe storage (or housing the occasional child wizard), but it can actually be the perfect space for a reading nook. Removing the stud wall, if there is one, and slotting in a low bench or chair, a reading lamp, and heaps of soft cushions can turn the space from an underutilized dust trap into a magical reading spot. Use the tallest end of the space to install your seating and the tricky, narrow end of the wedge to tuck in a few bookshelves. Now you've made the most of every scrap of floor space and created a fun hideaway for children and adults alike.

9

Wish Happiness for Others

A few years ago, an engineer named Chade-Meng Tan started to research ways to increase levels of happiness and emotional intelligence at work. The system he developed, Search Inside Yourself, was initially just for his colleagues, but it is now a globally recognized program. At its heart is a very simple secret to happiness. The best way to improve your own sense of well-being, says Tan, is to practice compassion. In other words, if you wish for other people to be happy, you will become happier, too. Dive into this chapter to discover how kindness can be contagious—and how it can make not just your home but your community a sweeter place for all.

The Secret Is Out

In many ways it seems counterintuitive to seek out happiness by wishing it for others, but the more I thought about it, the more it made sense. There is a certain selfless pleasure in acts of generosity, and taking the focus off yourself is bound to have a trickle-down effect on your own levels of joy. By wishing for others to be happy and acting on the impulse to be generous with your time, love, and money when possible, you can, in return, bask in the reflected glow of their happiness.

A scientific study led by researcher Soyoung Q. Park at the Department of Psychology at the University of Lubeck seems to back up this concept. In an experiment to test the link between generosity and happiness, two groups of volunteers were given a sum of money. Half were told to spend it on a treat for themselves while the other half were told to spend it on a treat for someone else. Those who spent the money on others later reported higher levels of happiness.

"Taking the focus off yourself is bound to have a trickle-down effect on your own levels of joy."

Eight Acts of Kindness to Boost Your Mood

Generosity means more than just spending money, though. Sometimes, small acts of kindness and thoughtfulness are just as effective as going out and buying a gift for someone. Here are eight ways to consider the happiness of others and share a little love.

1 Cook someone their favorite meal

Taking the time to prepare and cook someone their favorite meal will surely spread happiness—I know I am always ridiculously grateful if someone offers to cook for me. If you have culinary skills, share them widely and freely.

"There is a certain selfless pleasure to be found in acts of generosity."

2 Send thank-you letters

Handwritten thank-you letters are a joy to receive, so write them to friends and family whenever the situation warrants. Treat yourself to some beautiful notepaper or some pretty cards and make sure you send your notes promptly after someone sends you a gift or does something nice for you. In particular, encourage children to remember to send thank-you notes to relatives— especially those from older generations.

3 Invite someone for the holidays if you know they don't have family nearby

If you hear that a work friend or neighbor will be spending the holidays or a weekend alone, invite them over to share a meal with you and involve them in your own family's celebrations. If they don't have their own family nearby, they might be delighted to join in with your festivities. If you feel shy about inviting them, don't be; they can easily say a polite no if they would rather be alone, but even just offering is an act of kindness.

4 Do someone else's chores for them

If you notice that someone is having a really bad week, sprinkle a little happiness by doing a couple of their chores for them. I know that if someone offered to do the vacuuming and cleaning for me one week, I would be over the moon, so I can vouch for the effectiveness of this one.

5 Sort through your clothes and give everything you no longer wear to charity

If you have clothes, shoes, or bags gathering dust in the back of your closet, have a good clear-out and take everything you no longer wear to a local thrift store (see page 40). Allowing someone else to benefit from something you no longer need is easy, and it will make you feel good to know someone else can make use of it.

6 Bake a cake for someone

If you make an excellent lemon drizzle cake and you know it's your friend's favorite, don't wait until her birthday to make her one—surprise her with it on an ordinary weekday or whenever you think she might need a little encouragement.

"Make it a habit to vocalize positive or generous thoughts and you will spread cheer wherever you go."

7 Share a compliment

Noticing your friend's haircut is a tiny thing for you to do, but it could give her a big boost. Make it a habit to vocalize positive or generous thoughts and you will spread cheer wherever you go.

8 Go out of your way to see older relatives

If you have elderly relatives who live alone, invite them over for dinner, ask them about themselves, and listen to their stories. In the rush of everyday life it can be easy to overlook spending time with aunts, uncles, or grandparents, but they are the closest link you have to your own history, so treat them with kindness and respect and you will gain as much, if not more, from the interaction than they will.

Everybody Needs Good Neighbors

Where better to start in your quest to wish happiness for others than in your own community? I am lucky to live in a wonderful village where the concept of being a good neighbor is highly prized. The street I live on is particularly tight-knit and my lovely neighbors generously sprinkle small kindnesses around. They keep an eye on the house for me when I am out at work, put my garbage bins out for collection when I forget, and are always there for a chat if I need them to be. If you want to create a similar street spirit, treat your neighbors as you would your own family, and the sympathetic acts will boomerang back to you, I promise. Here are a few ways to be a good neighbor.

Offer to cut someone's lawn

If you live on a street with adjoining lawns, offer to mow your next-door neighbor's grass when you cut your own. They will probably be delighted, and they might even return the favor for you one day. But do check first— avid gardeners might not take kindly to someone taking over their favorite task.

Welcome new neighbors

Moving can be a stressful experience and it often falls to the new neighbors to introduce themselves to the existing residents of the street, which can be a bit nerve-racking. Make it easier for new neighbors by popping a welcome card in the mailbox when they arrive and by making the effort to say hello to them first.

Start a book-exchange library

There is an unused telephone box in my village that has been converted into a neighborhood lending library. It runs on an honesty system, whereby anyone can take a book for free and replace it with a book they no longer want or need. I absolutely love it, and it is very easy to set up. If there isn't an obvious communal area on your street for such a thing, try a small weather-proof book box in your front yard, or turn an old-fashioned mailbox into a mini lending library.

"Where better to start in your quest to wish happiness for others than in your own community?"

Support local events

If your local schools, youth groups, churches, arts centers, or local sporting teams put on performances or other events, make the effort to go along and encourage them. A lot of work can go into local events, and if only a handful of people turn up, it can be a little disappointing for all those who volunteer their time to make them happen. Turning up is a small act of kindness that is also a great way to meet your neighbors and show your moral support. Who knows, you might discover a surprising aptitude for singing along the way.

Make a handmade card

When I was a child my sisters and I always used to make handmade birthday cards for our elderly next-door neighbor. One year we ran out of time, so we sent her a regular store-bought card instead. When we saw her next she thanked us for the card but declared that she preferred the scrappy, glue-and-glitter-covered handmade ones, and she then produced a box filled with every card we had ever made her. After that, we reverted to making her birthday card every year. If you have a neighbor who would appreciate a handmade card, take the time to make one, or help your children make one.

Offer to look after your neighbor's home, pets, or plants while they are away

If your neighbors are planning a summer trip, put their minds at ease by offering to keep an eye on their home for them while they are away. Whether that involves collecting the mail, watering their prize tomato plants, or feeding their goldfish, it's a small gesture of the type that can really help community life blossom. Plus, your grateful neighbors might just offer to help you in exchange the next time you go away.

Share skills

Do you have a secret skill? Perhaps you are a guerrilla knitter, or maybe you are a champion banjo player? If so, don't keep it to yourself but offer your skills to anyone in your neighborhood who you think might be keen to learn. This doesn't mean you have to put a sign up in the window or take your banjo from door to door to spread the word. But if someone expresses an interest in a hobby of yours, offering to teach them or sharing some of your time or materials to get them started is a very kind thing to do.

Deliver holiday cards (or cookies) in person

I always try to pop a holiday card through the doors of my closest neighbors each year—it is a fun way to keep in touch, and I love to receive cards back, too. I also like to bake, so I make a batch of festive gingerbread cookies and, around a week or so before the holidays, I deliver them along the street. It is a nice way to chat with neighbors who I perhaps haven't seen for a while, and the cookies usually seem to be well received (or my neighbors are too polite to say otherwise). It is an easy thing to do and it makes me feel happy and festive to think that I am handing out a little bit of cheer along with the gingerbread.

It Takes a Village

Relationships are essential for our happiness at home, and slowing down and cultivating strong connections with your family, partner, or roommates is crucial when you are all sharing a living space. A major ongoing research project undertaken by the Harvard Study of Adult Development has followed hundreds of men for nearly eighty years (they started the study in 1938) and found that close relationships, more than money or fame, are what keep people happy throughout their lives. The research showed that close personal ties help delay mental and physical decline, and are better predictors of long and happy lives than social class, IQ, or even genetics. Here's how to build up your relationships at home.

Design your living room for conversation

It is too easy to design your living area around the TV, and many of us fall into this trap. If you think instead about designing your living room for conversation, however, you will be much more likely to use the space for chatting and relaxing, rather than just watching TV as a default behavior. All it might take is a quick design tweak, such as angling two sofas to look at each other, rather than having them both facing the TV, or making sure that each family member has his or her own dedicated space in a living room, so everyone will feel comfortable and want to spend time there instead of disappearing to their rooms every evening.

"Close relationships, more than money or fame, are what keep people happy throughout their lives."

Share meals at the dinner table

Sitting at the table to eat dinner together is a good way to make sure that you connect with family and friends at least once a day. If your dining table tends to be a magnet for clutter and you find yourself grabbing meals on the go or in front of the TV, make a point of keeping that space clear so you can sit down properly to eat in the evening. If you and your partner, children, or roommates tend to be out at different times in the evening, decide on one day a week when you will all agree to be in and make it a fixed weekly dinner date.

Take turns choosing a weekend activity

If someone in your household is an avid gardener but you are more of a baker, try to take an interest in each other's hobbies and trade off choosing an evening or weekend activity that you can both be involved in. You might not have a particular aptitude for propagating plant cuttings, but spending a weekend doing something that you know is important to a loved one is a great way to build up or strengthen a relationship. Plus, it might turn out that gardening, cookie making, or watercolor painting isn't all that bad—you never know.

Share music

Taste in music is something that varies wildly from person to person, and you don't have to have identical musical likes and dislikes to be able to live companionably with someone. In fact, it can be fun to pass an evening introducing each other to your favorite new (or old) music and learning to appreciate the tastes of your nearest and dearest. This can also make for a pretty lively debate, particularly when it spans generations, but taking a few hours to find out what makes your partner, child, or roommate tick is always time well spent.

Man's Best Friend

The natural extension of looking after someone other than yourself is to look after a pet, and a number of medical studies have confirmed the therapeutic benefits of having pets at home. If you would love to have a dog or a cat—or a fish or a hamster—but aren't currently able to do so (perhaps you live in an apartment with no extra or outdoor space), there are still ways to get some of the joy and happiness that a furry companion can bring.

Offer to look after your neighbors' pets

If you know your neighbors are jetting off on vacation, volunteer to look after their pets for them (see page 126). You will be doing a kind deed at the same time as benefiting from spending time with a cat, dog, or goldfish.

"A number of medical studies have confirmed the therapeutic benefits of having pets at home."

"Borrow" a pet for regular walks

If you aren't able to commit to having a pet at home full-time, there are a number of websites that can connect you with local pet owners who need someone to help take care of their cats and dogs while they are at work or when they go away on weekends. Fill in your preferences and availability and you'll be matched with a grateful local pet owner.

Foster a pet

Rescue shelters sometimes need help fostering pets for short periods of time while they are waiting to be rehomed. If you think you would like to help out in this way, get in touch with your nearest animal charity organization and ask about the application process.

10

Unearth Happiness in the Garden

If you have ever stretched out in the gently dappled shade of a tree on a hot summer's afternoon—listening to the bees lazily humming nearby and the rustle of leaves overhead—you will not be at all surprised to learn that being in contact with nature has the power to make you happier and healthier. Carving out that time, however, can be tricky, especially if the great outdoors aren't quite at your fingertips. Here are some ways to bring it closer—to your very doorstep, in fact—and harvest its benefits for your home.

It can be hard to know where to start when it comes to designing and planting your own patch of garden, especially if you have never picked up a spade before and struggle to differentiate your annuals from your perennials. To find out how we can all make the most of our outdoor spaces and, more importantly, why we should, I quizzed Professor Alistair Griffiths, director of Science and Collections at the Royal Horticultural Society (RHS).

"Being in contact with nature has the power to make you happier and healthier."

First, I asked him what benefits gardening can have for our health and happiness. "I believe that gardens have the power to improve our physical and mental health," says Professor Griffiths, "and there is an increasing body of scientific evidence that also proves this . . . from improved mental health and reduced cardiovascular morbidity, obesity, and risk of type 2 diabetes, to improved pregnancy outcomes and reduced isolation."

How can a garden have such a powerful effect? Professor Griffiths explains that these health benefits are due to the fact that gardens provide "psychological relaxation and stress alleviation, increased physical activity, increased social interaction, and reduced exposure to air pollutants, noise, and excess heat."

But do we need to have a large outdoor space to reap the most rewards? Absolutely not, he says. "The key thing is to be out in nature and to get gardening—be it a few houseplants or a large garden."

Three Gardening Activities for Non-Gardeners

Ready to dig in? Here are a few ideas to get you going, even if you have never picked up a watering can before.

1 Start small

You don't need to have acres of land to become a gardener. In fact, it is often better to start small, as it gives you the freedom to experiment with different plants until you hit on a combination that works for you. "Start with containers or a very small plot of land," recommends Alistair, and choose plants that are easy to grow, such as perennial bulbs that will come up year after year in a container. The more you experiment, the more plants you will find that work well in your climate, and you can use those to create the foundation of your garden. "Build on successes and not failures," says Alistair.

2 Create an herb garden

Growing herbs is one of the easiest ways to turn yourself into a gardener, as they are quick, simple, and fun to grow. Whether you take over a sunny kitchen windowsill with a few pots or plant a container outside your kitchen door, choose herbs that you love to cook with and scents that you enjoy. If you plant them outside, use them to line a path or place them close to the front door, so you can brush past them each time you leave the house and release some of that delicious herby scent. The following herbs are all good to start with: rosemary (*Rosmarinus officinalis*), sage (*Salvia officinalis*), chives (*Allium schoenoprasum*), mint (*Mentha*), and basil (*Ocimum basilicum*).

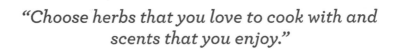

"Choose herbs that you love to cook with and scents that you enjoy."

3 Grow your favorite food

"Food is a great way to get people engaged with gardening," says Alistair, and I have to agree; there is nothing more satisfying than picking your own fresh strawberries in the height of summer. They often taste better than anything you can buy, and you feel a rush of self-satisfaction when you offer them to friends and family.

The golden rule with growing fruits and vegetables at home is just to grow whatever you love to eat; it sounds like a small feat, but it is easy to get carried away. You could grow a very pretty crop of runner beans, for example, because you like the way the delicate scarlet flowers and bright-green peapods look as they scramble up a tepee frame, but if you don't particularly enjoy eating or cooking with green beans then the crop will be wasted and you will run out of enthusiasm for it pretty quickly. Stick instead to growing fruits and vegetables you adore, be that strawberries, tomatoes, corn, lemons, or peppers, and you will create a harvest that's practical as well as pretty. The following are all great crops for non-gardeners to start with.

"The golden rule with growing fruits and vegetables at home is just to grow whatever you love to eat."

Fresh strawberries

These couldn't be less intimidating to grow. Buy a small plant early in the season—almost any garden center will sell them—pop it in a container or hanging basket, keep it well watered, and wait for your strawberry harvest to arrive in late summer. Invite friends over to share them and practice your casual, "Oh, these? I just grew them."

Ripe tomatoes

Again, buy a small plant early in the season and put it in a container or a patch of warm ground for a crop of tomatoes in late summer. Or, if you have a warm windowsill and some patience, you can grow your own tomatoes for free by squeezing the seeds from the center of a tomato into a pot of gardening soil. With a little care and a dash of luck, they will sprout into tiny shoots, which will turn into small plants, and then bigger plants, until they are ready to transfer to the garden in late spring.

"Gold" potatoes

Did you know that if you toss a "seed potato"—a leftover piece of potato—into a large bag of potting soil, it will grow a new crop of delicious potatoes under the surface? It is a great trick and a good harvest to get children involved in, as it's fun to pull up the leafy plant stems to reveal the little nuggets of potato "gold."

An idea for little gardeners

Gardening does take patience, so if you want to get children interested, choose a plant that is quick to grow and fun to eat. "Try growing seeds that germinate very quickly and which they can eat immediately," Alistair suggests. Take a clean, hollowed-out eggshell and fill it with damp cotton wool. Sprinkle seeds carefully onto the cotton wool, then place the eggshell in a sunny spot and wait for your crop to appear!

How to Create an Outdoor Living Room

Now that we've seen how much growing your own plants can improve your mood, here's how to turn your garden into an outdoor living room, allowing you to enjoy those long summer days and warm nights.

Take your indoor style outside

If you want to relax, unwind, and socialize in the garden, you need to think about the space in much the same way as you would an indoor living room. Giving equal care to your outdoor décor as you would to your interior means thinking about seating, lighting, and accessories. Transform a garden bench into a soft sofa with a few sturdy cushions and blankets; draw up a low table as a handy perch for drinks, snacks, and magazines; and bring in color, pattern, and personality with accessories such as lanterns, bunting, and oversized floor cushions.

Create some shelter

Don't let inclement weather send you running indoors. Introduce some shelter to your outdoor space, such as a canopy made from sailcloth or a covered pergola, to allow you to stay outside come rain or shine. There's nothing better than listening to the sound of rain gently falling on a canvas roof when you are dry and snug underneath.

> *"If you want to relax, unwind, and socialize in the garden, you need to think about the space in much the same way as you would an indoor living room."*

Shed some light

Make your garden an enticing place to linger in the evenings by hanging up a string of lights or investing in a few garden lanterns to illuminate your outdoor space after dark. Tealights in glass jars or solar-powered string lights are good options for adding a soft glow. But don't go overboard with the lighting; you don't want to create a floodlit glare, and it's actually detrimental to local wildlife (not to mention your human neighbors) to have too much light outside. Stick to soft, romantic lighting for a mellow mood.

Make a fire

A happily crackling fire is lovely to gather around when the evenings draw in, and a small fire pit or portable fireplace can usually be squeezed into even the most compact outdoor space, as long as there is adequate ventilation. Pop some marshmallows onto a toasting fork, bring out steaming mugs of rich hot chocolate, and invite friends and family to share stories around the embers as the scent of wood smoke drifts into the night air. That beats a night indoors in front of the TV, doesn't it? Having a heat source will also allow you to continue using your outdoor space into autumn and start using it earlier in spring.

Paint garden fencing, sheds, and furniture

Most garden fences and sheds are treated with a wood stain in varying shades of brown and given little other consideration. But it is high time we started giving our boundary walls and yard structures just as much consideration as our indoor walls and furniture. If you update your fencing or shed with a tinted wood stain to complement your interior style, it will help bring your garden to life and knit your indoor and outdoor spaces together. To help you choose the best shade, think of your garden fencing as a backdrop for your flowers and plants. Dark gray tones will allow bright colors to pop, while lighter shades of gray or white will create the perfect foil for Mediterranean plants such as lavender (*Lavandula*), citrus varieties, and olive trees (*Olea europaea*).

How to Green Up an Urban Garden or Balcony

Don't have acres of outdoor space to garden? Not a problem. Some of the cleverest and most impactful gardens are small urban ones where creativity runs wild. Bonus: A small garden is much easier to manage. Here's how to squeeze every drop out of your urban garden or balcony and create a mini oasis in the heart of the city.

Grow a green screen

Fast-growing climbers are excellent in a city garden, as they can scramble up a boundary wall or fence and provide additional privacy as well as a living green wall to look out on. Bamboo is another good option for a balcony, as it doesn't need a wall to climb, so it can be planted in a trough and grown up against a railing to provide a soft green screen that will gently rustle and sway in the breeze.

Look up

If floor space is at a premium, you will need to maximize vertical space instead. A wall-hung planter is great for raising flowers off the ground—and you can use anything from a simple hanging basket to a more complex "living wall" arrangement. Plant stands or small tables will also help raise plant pots and create a multilayered feel in your outdoor space, making a virtue of a small garden area by creating a lush, jungly effect.

Create a scent garden

If space is limited in a city garden, go large on scent instead of size to set up a beautiful outdoor space that packs a punch. To turn your outdoor space into a sensory retreat, Alistair suggests choosing scented plants such as lavender (*Lavandula*) and fragrant climbers such as jasmine (*Jasminum*) and honeysuckle (*Lonicera*). Be aware that scented plants release their fragrance at different times of the day, so if you plan to use the space more in the evenings, choose night-scented plants such as evening primrose (*Oenothera biennis*).

Start a little tea garden

In a small garden, the plants you choose need to work hard to earn their space. Alistair suggests planting a small herb garden on a balcony or even in a window box to provide herbs and plants for making your own fresh tea. Mint (*Mentha*), chamomile (*Matricaria chamomilla*), and lemon balm (*Melissa officinalis*) would make lovely additions to your tea tin.

"Many dwarf or compact trees can be suitable for urban patios or terraces—just plant them in large pots."

Squeeze in a tree

Think you haven't got space for a tree? You might be surprised. Many dwarf or compact trees can be suitable for urban patios or terraces—just plant them in large pots. I have two dwarf apple trees in my small garden that are only 5 feet (1.5 m) tall, but they produce a good crop of full-sized apples in the autumn and an abundance of frothy pink blossoms in spring. I also have a dwarf pear tree in the small patch of garden in front of my house, and in the autumn it provides an amazing crop of fruit while in the spring it produces beautiful pure white blossoms that drift down to the ground in a soft confetti of petals. Ask for advice at your local plant nursery to find the right tree for your region, position, and soil type.

Join the Green Gym (It's Free!)

A Harvard Medical School study found that thirty minutes of intense gardening could burn as many calories as thirty minutes of weightlifting, jogging, or skiing. If you want to get fit while enjoying all the other benefits of being out in the garden, the following activities will all burn calories and help you shape up—no gym membership required!

Good (mild calorie burn)
- Planting seedlings or shrubs
- Raking the lawn
- Bagging up grass or leaves

Better (moderate calorie burn)
- Weeding
- Planting trees
- Mowing the lawn with an electric or gas mower

Best (now you're pumping iron)
- Chopping and splitting wood
- Mowing the lawn with a push mower
- Digging

NATURE IS THE BEST MEDICINE

While a vigorous gardening session will burn calories and get your blood pumping—you might be amazed to hear that even sitting in a chair and looking out at a green view can have a positive effect on your health. In the 1980s a scientist named Roger S. Ulrich ran an experiment on patients recovering from surgery in the hospital and discovered that those who were able to see trees from their window were discharged from the hospital faster, had fewer complications, and required less pain medication than those who only had a view of a brick wall.

Go Where the Wild Things Are

Thinking of others rather than ourselves is a proven shortcut to happiness (see pages 118–131), and a good way to do this outside is to consider whom you will be sharing your garden with. And by that I don't mean friends and family; I mean the wildlife that will also be making your tiny oasis their home.

Can looking after wildlife make us happy?

I went back to the RHS to ask Helen Bostock, senior horticultural advisor, if a wildlife-friendly garden could hold the key to happiness outdoors. She believes it can, for three main reasons.

1 "Firstly, there's the simple enjoyment of experiencing nature," says Helen. "A generation that is in danger of suffering 'nature deficit disorder' can be cured with a few hours out in the garden a week, listening to blackbirds or discovering all the insects that a little patch of long grass can hold."

2 Speaking of insects, a wildlife garden can also help keep pests at bay. "By reducing the amount of pesticide used and providing overwintering sites for ladybugs, lacewings, and so on, you can increase the number of natural predators in a garden, meaning pests don't get the upper hand," says Helen.

3 And finally, by creating a wildlife paradise in your back garden, you can do your bit to help support pollinating insects, such as bees and hoverflies, which are essential pollinators of many wildflowers, garden plants, fruits, and vegetables. "You can also create a refuge for species such as common frogs or house sparrows that may not be doing so well in the wider countryside," says Helen. Your little bit of garden can act as "an essential patch in a wider green mosaic, making it easier for wildlife to stay connected."

"So, yes, by gardening with wildlife in mind, gardeners reap various rewards," concludes Helen. "And, of course, so does the wildlife."

Top tips for creating a wildlife paradise

- Allow a patch of grass to grow long
- Build a small pond or water feature, ensuring wildlife can readily get in and out of the water
- Construct a log pile
- Make a bee hotel or a more elaborate bug hotel
- Plant a hedge to create a green corridor between you and the neighbors

- Design a pollinator-friendly plot or potted plant collection, packed with flowers for every month of the year
- Put up a bat box or bird box
- Make sure garden lighting is not too bright and doesn't cause light pollution
- Make a compost heap

HUG A TREE

Personally, I don't need an excuse to go for a walk in a forest or park; I have even been known to hug a tree on occasion. But if you need a little encouragement to get outdoors, consider, if you will, the wonderfully named concept of *Shinrin-yoku* or "forest bathing." Japanese scientists have been studying this phenomenon for several years, and they have discovered that spending time walking underneath a cool, leafy canopy can have an astonishingly positive effect on human health, including lowering blood pressure, boosting the immune system, and reducing stress levels.

While you might not be able to plant a forest in your backyard, the trickle-down effect of being out in any type of nature is hard to dispute. So get out there immediately and find yourself a tree to hug. And if you can't find one, plant one.

11

How to Be Smarter Than Your Smartphone

Much of this book is about the joy of reconnecting with simple pleasures: spending time with friends, savoring a quiet moment in a sunny armchair, or enjoying a good night's sleep. In an age when we are increasingly driven by technology, much happiness can be found when we unplug, disconnect, and appreciate the small everyday joys to be found in the so-called real world, as opposed to the virtual one. In the following pages, you'll learn how to shift your technology habits so you can be blissfully present "IRL"—which is, after all, the world where your favorite spaces, activities, and people all exist.

According to the American Psychological Association's "Stress in America" survey of 2017, increased usage of social media and the constant checking of phones among Americans has left people feeling increasingly disconnected and more stressed. If you worry that your smartphone use is starting to have a negative impact on your happiness, the following pages will show you how to reclaim your time and focus.

Take Back Control

Let me be clear: I am not advocating a return to a pre-tech era. Far from it. There is so much that is fun, creative, and entertaining about the online world. We are better connected than ever before and are able to bring the outside world into our homes in an instant. Online tools can make our lives easier, and there is much to gain from living in a connected world.

Problems can come, however, when the use of gadgets is taken to an extreme, such that our home is no longer a refuge from work, school, or outside pressures because we are inviting those things in via our constantly connected phones, tablets, and laptops. This can be a particular concern for children and teenagers who struggle to disconnect from the constant chatter of social media when they should be relaxing in the comfort and security of their family home. The solution is to find a way to embrace tech for everything positive it has to offer and then balance it with your offline world.

Be the boss

It's good to review the way you use your devices and social media platforms every now and again to ensure you are getting the very most out of them while being fully in charge of their roles in your life. The goal is to get to a point where you pick up your phone or tablet for a specific purpose—to read an online magazine, connect with friends, or stay updated with news—as opposed to finding yourself at its beck and call.

Take the tech quiz

| Y | N | Do you constantly check your phone while you are at home? |

| Y | N | Does checking your social media accounts sometimes make you feel stressed or anxious? |

| Y | N | Do you get your work emails directed to your phone, and do you check them frequently at home? |

| Y | N | Has your sleep suffered as a result of your phone use? |

| Y | N | Do you ever feel "tired but wired"? |

If you answered yes to any of these questions, read on to learn how to embrace tech for all it has to offer while keeping it firmly in balance with other elements of your home life. If you answered no to all of these questions, congratulations—you may skip the next section.

Five Ways to Outsmart Your Smartphone

 Sort your apps

I used to have a lot of apps scattered across my phone's home screen, but when a friend told me about the way she managed and organized the apps on her phone, I thought it was really smart and immediately followed her lead. Here's her secret.

- First, ask yourself if an app is helpful, useful, or adds something to your life or well-being. These might be a fitness tracking app, a meditation app, your music playlists, or a home decorating app, for example. Keep all of these on the front screen of your device so they are easily accessible.
- Next, put all of the apps that you decide are purely fun, and that you would like to use in moderation, on the second page. These could be your social media accounts, dating apps, or news sites, for example.
- Finally, any apps that have the potential to drain your time without bringing value and positivity to your day (games, gossip sites, and so on) get relegated to the last page on your device and, ideally, put into a folder.

If you sort your apps this way, each time you check your phone you will be greeted first by all the apps that help, support, and bring joy, and you will be less tempted to idly click on those that bring less positivity to your life and can potentially drain your time. This method really does help you get on top of which apps make you happy and which don't.

 Update your notifications

An instant way to take control of your device is to switch off notifications for any apps that are nonessential, such as social media accounts or email. That way, you can check in only when you want to, rather than being summoned by a notification the second a new message arrives in your inbox. If you still want to receive updates, look at the settings of each individual app—you can usually set them to send you updates just once a day, for example, and you can decide on a time and frequency that work for you.

Be out-of-office

3

During your "offline" hours, put an out-of-office notification on all your email accounts—both work and private—even if it's only for a few hours. We are used to doing this when we go on weeklong breaks, but you can get into the habit of doing it whenever you want to clear some free time outside of work hours. If you want to keep an evening or weekend free for a family event, for example, put an out-of-office notification on your email account to say that you won't be checking in until the next morning, and leave a phone number for any emergencies. This will start to set clear boundaries for those who are likely to contact you during home hours, and it will put your mind at rest so you can relax and enjoy your downtime.

Bring back the telephone table

4

If you find you are carrying your phone around the house with you and checking it constantly, you might want to ease your dependency a little. Try treating your phone as if it's a landline and always put it back in the same place when you are not using it. An entryway table is a good location, and if you ensure there is a charging cable or docking station set up, it will become second nature to leave your phone there when you walk through the door. That way, you can go check it whenever you want, but it will start to become a conscious decision rather than a subconscious reflex.

Supercharge your sleep

We all know we shouldn't check our phones or tablets in bed, but the reality is that many of us do. If you want to cut down on your phone use at bedtime, here are a couple of easy steps to help, plus three ways that your phone can actually help you to sleep.

- An overload of blue light from digital devices at night can wreak havoc on your sleep patterns (see page 55). If you can't quite bring yourself to banish your phone from the bedroom, at least switch the screen to nighttime mode in the evenings to reduce the levels of blue light.

- Using your smartphone as your alarm clock means it's the first thing you reach for in the morning, and the next logical step is to start checking your email and social media accounts before you're even out of bed. Get an old-fashioned alarm clock instead and store your phone away from your bed overnight. Choose a fun one that makes you happy, such as a birdsong alarm or a daylight alarm clock that will gently wake you up by mimicking a sunrise.

- Want to transform your phone from something that robs you of sleep to something that gives it back? Download a sleep app to help soothe you to sleep at night. There are lots of great sleep apps out there that you can program to play comforting sounds or even read you a bedtime story as you drift off, and most will automatically shut down after thirty minutes or so, when you are hopefully sound asleep.

- Want to know exactly how much sleep you are getting each night? Invest in a sleep-tracking wristband to wear overnight and it will track your sleep patterns and download the information onto an app for you to review the next day. This will tell you how many times you woke in the night, as well as log any patterns of restlessness, which can indicate a problem you can look at tackling, such as an overheated bedroom or too much surrounding noise.

- If you struggle to switch off the background chatter and worries that race through your mind at night, there are a raft of really great guided meditation apps available that you can download to your phone to help you clear some headspace before bedtime.

Reclaim Your Leisure Time

If you find yourself aimlessly scrolling through social media apps or emails before you have even stepped out of bed in the morning and want to break the habit, it can help to think about what you could gain by getting this time back. Rather than spending twenty minutes reading about what the latest reality TV stars are up to, you could use that time to do any of the following instead.

20 minutes in the morning

- Drink a leisurely cup of tea while reading a book in your favorite chair.

- Sit outside feeling the sun on your face as you wake up slowly.

- Spend 20 minutes longer getting ready.

- Listen to a podcast or the radio.

- Have a coffee and a croissant at a café on the way to work, rather than a rushed slice of toast at home.

- Sleep! Enjoy more glorious sleep.

20 minutes in the evening

- Chat on the phone with a friend.

- Putter in the garden.

- Listen to a guided meditation app.

- Read a few chapters of a good book.

- Go for a quick run or bike ride.

- Dedicate the time to a hobby.

MAKE IT FUN
The carrot is always more enticing than the stick, so if you want to impose a daily tech limit for children, try rewarding them with a sticker on a chart each time they stay within the limit you have set. When the chart fills with stickers, offer a prize. Praising them for having self-control is a good way to help them work toward something they really want. (This reward system also works for adults.)

Rediscover Connection

Want to dial down the amount of time you and your family spend online at home and reconnect with simple pleasure in the offline world? Here's an idea.

Send real mail instead of emails

Why not relearn the joy of letter writing? Coming home to find a letter or small package has to be one of the best little treats there is. Link up with a friend or relative, or choose a friend you haven't seen in a while and send them a trinket out of the blue. This is a great activity for children to get involved with, too.

Here are some suggestions for good (small and light) things to wrap up and send.

For children

- Stickers
- Cheerfully patterned socks
- Pretty hair clips
- Fun stationery
- Paper airplane kit
- Small card game
- Small magic trick
- Pins, badges, or brooches
- Appliqué patches
- Key ring
- Packet of quick-grow vegetable seeds
- Origami paper
- Sunflower seeds
- Small paperback book

For adults

- Packet of hot chocolate or luxury tea
- Soft, colorful socks
- Paperback book
- Pretty notebook
- Nail polish
- Bar of nice chocolate
- Colorful pens
- Lip balm
- Packet of flower seeds
- Soothing face mask
- Pretty postcard
- Small print to frame

Bibliography and Further Reading

American Psychological Association. "Stress in America: Coping with Change," Stress in America™ Survey, 2017, www.apa.org/news/press/releases/stress/2017/technology-social-media.PDF (accessed August 1, 2017).

bloomon, www.bloomon.co.uk.

Carruthers, H. R., J. Morris, N. Tarrier, and P. J. Whorwell. "The Manchester Color Wheel: Development of a Novel Way of Identifying Color Choice and Its Validation in Healthy, Anxious and Depressed Individuals," *BMC Medical Research Methodology* 10, no. 12 (2010). (Copyright note: © Carruthers et al; licensee BioMed Central Lt., 2010. This article is published under license to BioMed Central Ltd. This is an Open Access article distributed under the terms of the Creative Commons Attribution License [https://creativecommons.org/licenses/by/2.0/] which permits unrestricted use, distribution, and reproduction in any medium, provided the original work is properly cited.)

Dove, Roja, www.rojadove.com.

Farrow & Ball, www.farrow-ball.com.

The Fragrance Foundation, fragrancefoundation.org.uk.

Hamer, M., E. Stamatakis, and A. Steptoe. "Dose-Response Relationship Between Physical Activity and Mental Health: The Scottish Health Survey," *British Journal of Sports Medicine* 43 (2009): 1111–1114.

Harvard Medical School. "Calories Burned in 30 Minutes for People of Three Different Weights," www.health.harvard.edu/diet-and-weight-loss/calories-burned-in-30-minutes-of-leisure-and-routine-activities (accessed August 1, 2017).

Harvard Study of Adult Development, www.adultdevelopmentstudy.org.

Haviland-Jones, J., H. Hale-Rosario, P. Wilson, and T. R. McGuire. "An Environmental Approach to Positive Emotion: Flowers," *Evolutionary Psychology* 3, no. 1 (2005): 104–132.

Neom Organics, www.neomorganics.com.

Park, S. Q. et al. "A Neural Link Between Generosity and Happiness," *Nature Communications* 8 (2017), no. 15964.

The Royal Horticultural Society, www.rhs.org.uk.

Saxbe, D. E., and R. L. Repetti. "No Place Like Home: Home Tours Correlate with Daily Patterns of Mood and Cortisol," *Personality and Social Psychology Bulletin* 36 (2010): 71–81.

Search Inside Yourself, siyli.org.

The Sleep Council, sleepcouncil.org.uk.

The Sleep Council's Bed Buyer's Guide, www.sleepcouncil.org.uk/wp-content/uploads/2016/11/BBG-website-view.pdf (accessed December 6, 2017).

Takenaka, K., and B. C. Wolverton. *Plants: Why You Can't Live Without Them*. New Delhi: Roli Books, 2010.

Tan, Chade-Meng. *Search Inside Yourself: The Unexpected Path to Achieving Success, Happiness (and World Peace)*. New York: HarperOne, 2012.

Ulrich, R. S. "View Through a Window May Influence Recovery from Surgery," *American Association for the Advancement of Science* 224, no. 4647 (1984): 420–421.

Welsh, J. "Smell of Success: Scents Affect Thoughts, Behaviors," www.livescience.com/14635-impression-smell-thoughts-behavior-flowers.html (accessed December 7, 2017).

Wolverton, B. C. *How to Grow Fresh Air: 50 Houseplants that Purify Your Home or Office*. London: Weidenfeld and Nicolson, 2008.

Index

Acknowledgments

I would like to say a huge thank you to the team at Octopus for taking me under their wing and turning my spark of an idea into reality; particular thanks to Stephanie Jackson for understanding my idea right from the start and giving me the go ahead, to the lovely Ella Parsons for her calm editing skills and endless patience, and to the super-talented Juliette Norsworthy for weaving her design magic and turning my ideas into a beautiful little gem of a book. I am so grateful to Cathryn Summerhayes at Curtis Brown for putting me in touch with such a talented team.

A huge thank you to all of the scientists, researchers, and experts who took time out of their busy schedules to answer my many questions, and for contributing their knowledge and skill to this project. Special thanks are owed to Dr. Bill Wolverton, Kozaburo Takenaka, Joa Studholme, Lisa Artis, Nicola Elliott, Roja Dove, Stuart Fenwick, Professor Alistair Griffiths, Dr. Phyllis Zee, Kasper Iversen, and Helen Bostock; this book couldn't exist without your research, talent, and knowledge, and it is a privilege to have this opportunity to share your work further.

Debbie Powell's beautiful illustrations bring so much life to this book; I owe you many thanks for each and every one of your bright, joyful little drawings.

Finally, thank you to all my friends and family, who have put up with me talking about this book nonstop, for entertaining my endless questions, encouraging me when all the late nights and weekends were starting to overwhelm, and generally being wonderfully, brilliantly supportive. Special thanks to Charlotte Duckworth and Susie Ewert-James, for the knowledge, encouragement, friendship, and wine you provided along the way.

Picture Credits